SPIRITUAL GUIDES

ANNICE CALLAHAN, R.S.C.J.

SPIRITUAL GUIDES
FOR TODAY

Evelyn Underhill, Dorothy Day, Karl Rahner
Simone Weil, Thomas Merton, Henri Nouwen

CROSSROAD • NEW YORK

1992

The Crossroad Publishing Company
370 Lexington Avenue, New York, NY 10017

Printed in the United States of America
Typesetting output: TEXSource, Houston

Library of Congress Cataloging-in-Publication Data

Callahan, Annice, 1945-
    Spiritual guides for today : Evelyn Underhill, Dorothy Day, Karl
Rahner, Simone Weil, Thomas Merton, Henri Nouwen / Annice Callahan.
        p.   cm.
    Includes index.
    ISBN 0-8245-1109-3 (pbk.)
    Spiritual life—History of doctrines—20th century. I. Title.
    BV4490.C35   1991
    248'.092'2—dc20   91-17452
                                                                   CIP

To my R.S.C.J. communities at
72 Brunswick, Toronto,
and
100 Cushing, Cambridge, Massachusetts,
with whom I shared life and faith
during the writing of this book

Contents

Acknowledgments

Portions of the chapter "Thomas Merton (1915-1968): A Living Mystery of Solitude" have been previously published in "Traditions of Spiritual Guidance: Thomas Merton as Spiritual Guide" in *The Way* 28 (April 1988): 164-76.

Portions of the chapter "Karl Rahner (1904-1984): Theologian of Everyday Christian Life" have been previously published in "Traditions of Spiritual Guidance: Karl Rahner's Insights for Spiritual Direction" in *The Way* 29 (October 1989): 3341-48.

Photograph of Dorothy Day is included courtesy of the Memorial Library Archives of Marquette University, Milwaukee, Wisconsin.

Photograph of Thomas Merton is included courtesy of the Merton Archives of the Abbey of Gethsemani, Trappist, Kentucky.

Photograph of Evelyn Underhill is included with the permission of Morehouse Publishing, Wilton, Connecticut.

Photograph of Simone Weil is included with the permission of Librairie Arthème Fayard, Paris, France.

Foreword

Spiritual Guides for Today is the fruit of Annice Callahan's ability to combine scholarship with writing that is warm, insightful, inspirational, and invitational. One has the feeling that each of the women and men whom she proposes to us as guides for our own journey in faith has not been a stranger along the passage of her own pilgrimage.

Callahan's published doctoral thesis, entitled *Karl Rahner's Spirituality of the Pierced Heart*, as well as an edited volume of her essays, *Spiritualities of the Heart*, give more than a hint as to what is an important source in her own spiritual journey. In the Introduction to *Spiritual Guides for Today*, she indicates that the spirituality of Karl Rahner has provided a lens for the study of the six women and men whom she has chosen. Particular attitudes of heart, however, are highlighted, which bespeak values that she feels have meaning and motivation for us as well.

At the same time, the reader does not get the impression that the author has written her own spiritual biases into the lives of these contemporary women and men. She presents them to us in a way that lets them speak for themselves. Her interpretations are not forced nor are they presented in homiletic fashion. The concluding paragraphs at the end of each section present her own distillation of the way these writers can be spiritual guides for us as we struggle to live a faith that challenges us to discover God in our own hearts, in others, and in the world. Moreover, in this very discovery we detect that such a finding of God will not be outside of situations of suffering and sorrow that compel and command us to take our own stand in compassion and solidarity.

The six women and men whom Annice Callahan chooses as spiritual guides for our times were often, interestingly enough, guides for one another as well. It is important not to set aside the Introduction where these connections are made. In this section, the author also indi-

cates themes and points of emphasis around which their writings and
concerns converged.

Spiritual Guides for Today is a book that deserves more than one
reading. The content is rich and rewarding but not exhaustive. The
author writes with an economy of words that leaves the reader wishing
for more. Perhaps this is designedly so. It is almost as though she wants
us to discover for ourselves the treasures that we will inevitably find if we
meet these women and men in their own words and not only through the
prism of her personal perceptions. The endnotes of each chapter offer
wonderful enticements for such deeper exploration, and a selected list of
the author's own writings as well as other readings presents an incentive
to journey further in the company of these very human, humble, and
sometimes fragile friends of God.

MARGARET BRENNAN, I.H.M.
Regis College, Toronto

Preface

I want to thank my family, who were my first spiritual guides. Then I want to thank the Religious of the Sacred Heart for the spiritual guidance and support I have received, first as a student and now as a member of the congregation. In particular, I am grateful for the interest, patience, and encouragement of my community at 72 Brunswick Avenue in Toronto, with whom I live, and my community at 100 Cushing Street in Cambridge, Massachusetts, with whom I lived during my semester research leave in the spring of 1989. At the same time, I am indebted to Regis College for the granting of my research leave, to George Schner, S.J., who was dean at the time, for his encouragement to take the leave at that time, and to Jean-Marc Laporte, S.J., our current dean, who was a critical reader for rough drafts of the chapters on Merton, Nouwen, and Rahner. I am grateful to the Association of Theological Schools of the United States and Canada for their generous grant that made this research possible during my semester leave from Regis College in the spring of 1989. In particular, I am indebted to Dr. Francine Cardman of Weston College, my mentor for this project, who read critically my chapter manuscripts on Day, Underhill, and Weil. My thanks also go to the University of Dayton Library, which offered me invaluable assistance during the summer of 1990. I am indebted to Phillip M. Runkel for the tapes and articles by Dorothy Day and Thomas Merton that he sent me from the Marquette University Archives.

For a critical reading of my chapter on Evelyn Underhill, I thank Christopher Armstrong of the Vicarage in Cropthorne, Pershore, England, Grace Adolphsen Brame of Villanova University, Dana Greene of St. Mary's College of Maryland, and Joy Milos, C.S.J., of Gonzaga University.

For helpful suggestions on my chapter on Dorothy Day, I thank Robert Coles of Harvard University, William D. Miller, formerly of Marquette University, Catherine Mooney, R.S.C.J., of Yale University Divinity School, Jack Seery, S.J., of Haley House in Boston, and Mrs. Mary Wuller of St. Louis University.

I am grateful to Karl Rahner, S.J., for his availability and advice during the semester I spent in Innsbruck, Austria, in the spring of 1982. I want to thank my R.S.C.J. community in Innsbruck for their hospitality, encouragement, and support. I thank Frau Oeggl, Rahner's secretary at the time, for her help. I have taught Rahner's theology for five years and continue to be inspired by the depth and breadth of his faith vision, as well as by the integrity of his faith commitment. For valuable comments on my chapter on Karl Rahner, I am grateful to Rev. James C. Bacik of Corpus Christi Parish in Toledo, Anne Carr, B.V.M., of the University of Chicago Divinity School, Rev. John Galvin of Catholic University of America, and Brian O. McDermott, S.J., of Weston School of Theology.

For their collaboration on my chapter on Simone Weil, I acknowledge the following: Robert Coles, Leslie Fiedler of the State University of New York at Buffalo, Mary Rita Grady, C.S.J., of Regis College, Weston, Massachusetts, Margaret Guider, O.S.F., of Weston School of Theology, Dorothy McFarland of Leverett, Massachusetts, Eric Springsted of Illinois College, and Wilhelmina Van Ness of Leverett, Massachusetts.

I am grateful for the influence of Thomas Merton on my life. I began reading his books about thirty years ago. When I was a novice, I began a correspondence with him that lasted until his death. I have taught a course on Merton and include his books as units in other courses. For their help with my chapter on Thomas Merton, I want to thank the following: Anne Carr, B.V.M., Patrick Hart, O.C.S.O., of the Abbey of Gethsemani, George Kilcourse of Bellarmine College, and Brian O. McDermott, S.J.

I am grateful to Henri Nouwen for his friendship, inspiration, and support. Henri and I first met in Boston and have continued our relationship now that we are both in Toronto. My thanks to Martha Smalley, Joan Duffy, and the other members of the library staff at the Yale Divinity School for easy access to the Nouwen archives during my summer of research there in 1987. The Sisters of Mercy on Prospect Street offered me hospitality and the inspiration of their work with homeless children. I also want to thank Connie Ellis, Henri's secretary, for her help and our many exchanges on the phone. I assign Henri's books in my courses and they always receive a positive response. For their constructive remarks about my chapter on Henri Nouwen, I am indebted to the following: Robert Durback of Cleveland, John Mogabgab, editor of *Weavings*, and Susan Mosteller, C.S.J., of Daybreak l'Arche in Toronto.

I want to thank my students in my course on Spiritual Guides for Today, which I have taught several times. We have been learners together. I am humbled and awed by their enthusiasm, involvement, and transformation.

Frank Oveis has been an outstanding editor, providing the initial encouragement for this project and sustaining me with support. Phyllis Braceland, R.S.C.J., Claire Kondolf, R.S.C.J., and Anne Leonard, R.S.C.J., have given heroically of their time and energy reading the manuscript. Stephen LaCroix, C.S.B., helped significantly with the final editing. My sister, Aileen Callahan, prepared the expansive cover design, which captures the ability of these spiritual guides to shed light in darkness and to offer hope in our broken world.

Introduction

The expression "spiritual guide" suggests what in the East is called a "guru" and in the West is called a "spiritual director." In fact, spiritual direction can take place several ways — with a group or one-to-one, in person or by letter. Some spiritual guides are formal spiritual directors; others influence by their writings and the example of their lives. A spiritual guide is one who is led by the Spirit of God to help us be guided by the Spirit.

Spiritual guides for today point us toward our future in God. They invite us to get in touch with our own hearts in order that we may help others get in touch with theirs. They are symbols of the living God, revering their own mystery and revealing the mystery of God's love through their lives and writings.

Each of these spiritual guides lived certain attitudes of heart with which we can identify. An attitude of heart is a way of living a particular value. For example, gratitude is an attitude of heart that conveys the humble conviction of our need for others and for God in our lives. Trust is an attitude of heart that communicates faith in the strength of our personal relationship with ourselves, others, and God. Compassion is an attitude of heart that enables us to feel with others in their pain and joy by entering into their shoes, as it were, and seeing reality with their eyes. A person listening with compassion can mediate God's forgiving nearness in a tangible way.

This book explores the lives and writings of six contemporary spiritual guides: Dorothy Day, Thomas Merton, Henri Nouwen, Karl Rahner, Evelyn Underhill, and Simone Weil. Four of these are Roman Catholic, one Anglican, and one Jewish. Two are American, one is British, one is French, one is German, and one is Dutch. These three women and three men represent a cross-section of strands of the Judeo-Christian tradition.

Evelyn Underhill (1875–1941) was a British Anglican mystic and mystical theologian who was given an experiential knowledge of the mystery of God. She wrote books on mysticism and became one of England's leading authorities on the subject. She also became popular as a spiritual director and retreat director in the later part of her life.

Dorothy Day (1897–1980) was an American Roman Catholic journalist and co-founder of the Catholic Worker movement in the United States. She wrote on issues of social justice and concerns about bringing the gospel message to bear on the reality of daily life. Her common-law marriage, her abortion, her times in jail, and her conversion to Roman Catholicism enable many to identify with her search for God.

Karl Rahner (1904–84) was a German Jesuit theologian and *peritus* at the Second Vatican Council. His *Theological Investigations* plumbed the depths of the mystery of the Roman Catholic faith in light of the signs of the times, in particular its dialogue with contemporary science and scholarship. His theological insights into the practice of the Christian life in the world today are an example of the intrinsic relationship between spirituality and theology. He was a guide not only for his fellow theologians, but also for many others, including college students, women religious, and priests.

Simone Weil (1909–43) was a French Jewish philosopher and teacher of philosophy. Her efforts to live the lifestyle of afflicted people in factories and in the fields prepared her to live solidarity at a profound level. The controversial nature of many of her writings and the circumstances surrounding her death throw into relief her singleminded search for the truth.

Thomas Merton (1915–68) was an American Trappist monk whose writings have made accessible the story of his conversion to Roman Catholicism, his vocation to solitude, the renewal of monasticism in this century, the dialogue between Eastern and Western monasticism, and the struggle of contemplatives to become critics of society.

Henri Nouwen (1932–) is a Dutch clinical psychologist, pastoral minister, writer, and diocesan priest living at Daybreak, a l'Arche community in Toronto. His thoughts on conversion are born of his own struggle to live a life of shared faith in a community of handicapped people.

In the conclusions of five chapters, I indicate connections I make with Karl Rahner's spirituality, since his view has served as a lens for this study. At the end of each chapter is a list of suggested readings on each of the six writers. The endnotes are separate units so that the reader can read one chapter without skimming the book for abbreviated codes. In other words, I repeat initial entries in each chapter. At the end of the book is an index to facilitate references.

Connections

Some of these spiritual writers knew each other or at least knew of one another's work.

Dorothy Day was familiar with Simone Weil's work and enjoyed reading it.[1]

As well, she read Merton's *The Seven Storey Mountain*, and concluded that in the second part of the book he had "plunged himself so deeply in religion that his view of the world and its problems is superficial and scornful" (*Day*, 453). Dorothy Day then wrote to Thomas Merton in February 1959, sending him copies of the *Catholic Worker*. He replied in July 1959, supporting her nonviolent action of refusing to take shelter during civil defense drills in New York City. Merton began to see the social implications of living the Christian commitment, praising the *Catholic Worker* for its pacifist stand. About twenty of his articles, letters, and reviews were published in the *Catholic Worker*, including a version of "The Root of War Is Fear," which later appeared in *Seeds of Contemplation* and was revised for *New Seeds of Contemplation*.[2]

Like Merton in *Conjectures of a Guilty Bystander*, Day turned her gaze to national and international concerns in *On Pilgrimage: The Sixties*. In 1962, both Dorothy Day and Merton were part of the group that began the American Pax, a Catholic peace group that changed its name to Pax Christi in 1972. On November 8, 1965, Roger la Porte, claiming to be a Catholic Worker, burned himself to death in front of the United Nations building. Merton wrote to Dorothy in chagrin and disbelief that idealism could move a person to suicide. Dorothy had not even known la Porte, but was criticized harshly for his deed (*Day*, 478–79, 482–83).

Merton corresponded with Dorothy Day between at least 1959 and 1968.[3] In the early 1960s, he wrote several significant articles on war and peace for the *Catholic Worker* while Dorothy Day was still editor. As Gordon Zahn observed: "The special measure of admiration and affection he felt for Dorothy Day was inspired in great part by her willingness to go to jail for her convictions."[4] Although Merton said that only one or two people besides his abbot knew about his trip to the East, it turns out that Dorothy Day had announced it at the fifth annual conference of PAX.[5]

Urged by war protesters to leave the monastery to join them in the struggle, Merton wrote Dorothy to explore with her the possibility of his working as a missionary priest with American Indians. Dorothy urged him to stay where he was. Weeks before his death, Merton had assured her in a letter not to worry about his future, which did not include his being a political voice in the peace movement: "It is more and more clear to me that if I pretended to keep up with politics here and tried to utter profound judgments from my solitude I would be deceiving myself and perhaps others" (*Day*, 493–94).

On December 11, 1968, Dorothy received a telegram announcing Merton's death. That same month she wrote a tribute to her friend Merton, in which she quoted from his letters to her about his intention to stay a Trappist.[6] In an article she wrote on world peace Dorothy Day quoted a passage from Karl Rahner's book *The Christian Commitment* in which he talked about the growing importance of the new possibilities of organized human society.[7]

Thomas Merton recorded in his 1965 journal that he had read a biography of Simone Weil. He considered her mysticism basically authentic. He valued her critique of shallow personalism. He wrote an article on her, "Pacifism and Resistance in Simone Weil," which was later published in one of his books, and in which he underlined the significance of her thought in our time, her unsentimental and realistic love of peace, her rejection of the notion of war as an unavoidable fatality, her belief in nonviolent resistance: "Few writers have more significant thought than Simone Weil on the history of our times and a better understanding of our calamities."[8] Thomas Merton admired Simone Weil "whose ideas intrigued and challenged Merton's own mind and helped convert him to nonviolence."[9]

Merton corresponded with Karl Rahner. In 1964 he acknowledged his agreement with Rahner's notion of diaspora in *The Christian Commitment*, sending Rahner a copy of his own article on this subject. He was deeply affected by Rahner's use of the term "diaspora" to refer to the situation in which the church is not the dominant institution in society but rather a remnant. Merton adopted this term to predict that monks in the diaspora will be called upon to see their place in the world, which consists of a separation from and a dialogue with the world; monastic institutions in the diaspora must be more flexible and open to charismatic changes.[10] In *Seeds of Destruction*, he devoted a section to the diaspora in which he discussed the Christian in diaspora.[11]

In *The Genesee Diary*, Henri Nouwen noted that he was reading Evelyn Underhill's *The Mystics of the Church* with profit. He observed her insistence on the fact that mystics do not withdraw from the world but involve themselves creatively in the world. Ecstatic experiences can go hand in hand with practicality.[12]

On November 15, 1974, Nouwen quoted Dorothy Day in his talk on "Christianity and the Christ Room." He affirmed her suggestion that every Christian could designate a room for a guest to be welcomed.[13]

Nouwen wrote a book on Thomas Merton, calling him a contemplative critic; insisting that Merton is "one of the most important spiritual writers of our century."[14] On August 6, 1974, he recorded in his diary that he had been reading Merton's article on the Pasternak affair.[15] On August 11, he indicated that after his visit to Rochester, the passage from Merton's *Conjectures* about one of his trips to Louisville took on special meaning. At the corner of Fourth and Walnut, Merton was struck by the fact that all of us belong to God and to one another, even our solitude, so that others are not strangers but our own selves. Nouwen himself realized in Rochester how solitude had made him more sensitive to people's goodness and to the shared gift of grace.[16] On November 23, he reflected on Merton's influence since his death, since people emphasize different and sometimes contradictory aspects of his life and thought: some view him as a contemplative and others as a social critic, many describe him as a Christian monk while non-Christians take him as their model. Nouwen hailed him as a catalyst for us to find our way to God in the free space that Merton created by his ministry. On December 10, Nouwen recalled this anniversary of Merton's entrance into Gethsemani and death in Bangkok.[17] In reflecting on the ministry of the contemplative to make visible what one sees in prayer, Nouwen recalled that Merton had spoken of the contemplative life as a life of moving from the dark into open space.[18]

Comparisons

Some of the themes and points of emphasis of these six spiritual writers can be compared. Simone Weil and Evelyn Underhill, for example, were both drawn to impersonal symbols of God.

Both Evelyn Underhill and Simone Weil underwent significant shifts in their attitudes toward war and peace, Underhill toward pacifism and Weil away from it.

Both Underhill and Weil had a knowledge of and respect for early pagan Greeks, Underhill for Plotinus and Weil for Plato. In the Appendix to *Mysticism*, Underhill sketched a history of European mysticism beginning with Philo, including Plotinus and Porphyry (*Mysticism*, 454-56). Like Weil, she also turned to the East and included mention of Sufi or Mohammedan mysticism (*Mysticism*, 462). Underhill quoted Rabia, the Mohammedan contemplative called the "Moslem St. Teresa," the Hindu Kabir, and the pagan Plotinus.[19] Both Underhill and Rahner spoke of a mysticism for ordinary believers. Underhill called it a "practical mysticism" and Rahner a "mysticism of everyday life." Underhill's insistence on nonreligious, secular interests sounded like Rahner's theology of everyday things, which encouraged the cultivation of the habit of calm and quiet reflection through aesthetic and intellectual experience.[20]

Both Underhill and Rahner valued Ruysbroeck. She considered him the greatest mystic. Rahner copied a passage from him in an old notebook to which he returned often.[21]

In her preface to the twelfth edition of *Mysticism*, Underhill indicated changes she would have made in light of the development of her thought (*Mysticism*, vii-xi). In the French edition of *The Ascent to Truth*, Merton also indicated that he would have written it differently, discussing the unconscious, referring more to Scripture and the early church writers and less to scholasticism.[22] In fact, he revised the spiritual classic *Seeds of Contemplation* five times.[23]

Both Dorothy Day and Simone Weil identified with and were devoted to the poor. Dorothy wrote newspaper articles and Simone wrote philosophical essays about oppression.[24] They concentrated on identifying with the plight of workers and unemployed people. Dorothy actually joined workers for their sit-down strikes and supported them in the *Catholic Worker* (*Loneliness*, 204-22). Weil took a year to be a factory worker, but could not sustain the regime, either physically or psychologically. She observed in her essays that the workers' strike in Germany died down because there was a split between the factory workers and the unemployed, and she was led to evaluate the effectiveness of trade unions. She chose to belong to the class of unskilled women workers, the class most despised in the French factory system.[25]

Both Day and Weil put themselves in dialogue with communism. Weil belonged to a communist-dominated teachers' trade union. In many of her essays, she clarified and critiqued Marx and Marxism.[26] She was aware of Marx's critique of religion as the opium of the people. But his dialectical materialism was for her a religion lacking mysticism (*Oppression*, 163). Weil was one of the few who wrote on the role of the German Communist party just before Hitler's coming to power and the destruction of the working-class movement in Germany. Weil was a dissident who was never a member of the Communist party even though she may have considered joining for a time (*Writings*, 9, 95–96).

Both Day and Weil loved to go to Mass. Day went to Mass before and after her baptism; Weil would go to hear the music.[27]

Dorothy Day and Simone Weil both wrote for newspapers. Dorothy was a journalist all her life for different newspapers. Weil wrote for several newspapers while teaching at Le Puy. Between 1933 and 1934, Simone wrote "The Situation in Germany," an essay published as ten articles in leftist newspapers, on Hitler's rise to power and comintern politics (*Writings*, 91, 97–147).

Both Day and Weil were pacifists. Dorothy was an absolute pacifist who was consistent in her opposition to armed resistance, the atom bomb, and air-raid drills. Simone wrote essays between 1933 and 1940 on war and peace, reflecting her pacifist thought (*Writings*, 237–78). She did, however, participate in the Spanish civil war for a year. Both Day and Weil were opposed to air-raid drills as being militaristic. Day was unwilling to participate in air-raid drills and preferred to get arrested yearly in her nonviolent resistance to them (*Loneliness*, 263–73). Weil was conscious of the dehumanizing effects of air-raid shelters and air-raid warnings (*Oppression*, 119). By mid-1934, she decided to stop participating in political activities except during the campaign against civil defense exercises (*Writings*, 151).

Both Day and Weil kept journals. Dorothy kept journals of the retreats she made and of her everyday life, especially on her trips, such as to Cuba and Rome.[28] Simone kept a Factory Journal during 1934–35 when she was an unskilled factory worker (*Writings*, 155–226).

Both had spiritual guides for themselves. Dorothy was greatly helped by spiritual directors and retreat directors such as Joseph McSorley, C.S.P., and Father John Hugo. Simone was greatly helped by conversation and correspondence with Father Joseph-Marie Perrin. Both read avidly and had their favorite saints. Dorothy was more drawn to Teresa of Avila and Thérèse of Lisieux, and Simone to John of the Cross. Both quoted from Catherine of Siena. Both read and loved Dostoevsky.

Simone Weil wrote nothing on forgiveness, reconciliation, or community; Dorothy Day wrote much on community. Weil focused on the passion and death of Jesus; Day focused on the resurrection of Jesus.

Like Thomas Merton, Dorothy Day was a convert to Catholicism and immediately absorbed the best of Catholic literature. She, Karl Rahner, and Thomas Merton wrote and spoke of the moral reprehensibility of nuclear war and the absolute necessity of nuclear disarmament. Their global concerns around this issue mark them as spiritual guides for today, whose personal relationship with God has socio-political implications and responsibilities in the public sphere.

Both Weil and Merton quoted John of the Cross, the spiritual guide who wrote so powerfully about the dark night of the soul, but who also wrote poignantly about the living flame of love.[29] Evelyn Underhill, Karl Rahner, and Simone Weil challenge us to an intellectual honesty about our faith. Weil could not imagine God to be the god of battle and bloodshed portrayed by the Old Testament, taking sides and seeking vengeance.

Rahner and Merton can be called mystics for our time.[30] Both treated similar topics: issues of peace and war, priesthood and religious life in upheaval, and ecumenism. They had different points of emphasis. As a monk, Merton was very concerned about the future of monasticism; as a theologian, Rahner was very concerned about the future of the church. Having renounced the world, Merton was interested in entering into a life-giving dialogue with the world; Rahner was interested in portraying the world as a world of grace, the place of God's presence. Merton was interested in the East-West dialogue; Rahner was interested in Christianity's dialogue with atheism and with Judaism.

As we read these chapters, perhaps we can ask ourselves: How is this person a spiritual guide for me? Who are other spiritual guides in my life? For whom am I a spiritual guide? How can I respond more openly to the Spirit guiding me interiorly in the movements and deepest desires of my heart as well as in events of daily life? How can I respond more lovingly to the people whom God has entrusted to me? Let us take a moment to give thanks for the spiritual guides in our lives and for those to whom we are spiritual guides.

1
EVELYN UNDERHILL

(1875–1941)

Pathfinder for Our Way to God

EVELYN UNDERHILL, English poet, novelist, and mystical theologian, was born in 1875. Her many books on mysticism and prayer made her a leading authority in her time. Nominally Anglican for many years, she was drawn to the mystical and sacramental life of Roman Catholicism but repelled by its intellectual narrowness and thwarted by the anticlerical bias of Hubert Stuart Moore, whom she married in 1907. This was the year of the encyclical *Pascendi*, which condemned modernism. In 1921 Baron Friedrich von Hügel, a pro-modernist Roman Catholic layman, became her spiritual director. He encouraged her ecclesial instinct and need for communal worship and prayer. Gradually, Underhill herself began, in spite of poor health, to give retreats and spiritual direction to her fellow Anglicans. Toward the end of her life, just before World War II began, she became an active pacifist.

Underhill's mysticism revealed divine transcendence in the homey details of daily life. She saw self-sacrificing love of neighbor as the acid test of one's love of God. Prayer is social and incarnational, involving communal worship and service to the poor. It is contemplative, nourished by times of silence and retreat away from the duties and distractions of one's normal surroundings.

Underhill contributed significantly to the theology of mysticism. She translated some of the major medieval mystical authors into modern English with scholarly introductions and notes. Steeped in the lives and works of many Christian mystics, she delighted, too, in non-Christian mystic traditions. She was largely self-taught, yet was made a fellow of King's College, Cambridge, in 1928, and received an honorary doctorate in divinity from the University of Aberdeen in 1938.

Underhill's breadth and clarity of vision, her depth of insight, and her own kindness qualify her as a pathfinder in the mystic way. Hers was not only the academic knowledge of texts, but also the experiential knowledge of God. This chapter treats her spirituality under five aspects: unitive knowledge, living the spiritual life, growth in prayer, cultivation of the spirit of worship, and renewed commitment to the church.

Unitive Knowledge of Mysticism: Experience and Interpretation

Evelyn Underhill's knowledge of mysticism was unitive in that her interpretation of others' mystical experiences was based on her own. In her major work, *Mysticism*, 1911, she claimed that mysticism alone proves the existence of the absolute, and she proposed a way of knowing and attaining mysticism (*Mysticism*, 23–24, EU-Greene 5).[1] Not satisfied with William James's description of "marks of the mystic," she offered four of her own: mysticism is practical rather than theoretical, its aims are entirely spiritual, its business and method is love, and it entails a definite, organic life-process of conversion and transformation that is not self-seeking.[2] Mysticism is a loving, intuitive knowledge of self, God, others, and the world, based on personal religious experience.

Underhill saw mystics as theologians, in the sense that they both experience the mysteries of faith and reflect on these mysteries as lived. Her reflection allowed spirituality a diversity of symbolism to suit different lives: the mystic quest, the marriage of the soul, and spiritual alchemy. She claimed her own authority. She preferred her own classification of stages — the self's awakening, initial purification, illumination, final purification, and union with God — to the traditional threefold division. She was competent and sensitive in delicate areas, such as the psychic phenomena often linked with mystical experience.[3]

Underhill was a scholar, immersed in scholarly and critical dialogue.[4] She could express the genius and the experiences of the mystics to others. In *Practical Mysticism*, 1915, she offered the following definition: "Mysticism is the art of union with Reality" *(Practical*, 3). An act of simplifying prepares us for mystical experience. This involves recollection, which is the discipline of attention, and purgation, which simplifies the affections, the will, and the heart. Mysticism brings about a spiritual fruition since it is life-giving for others (*Practical*, 30, 32, 45,

67, 90-91, 103, 167-69). The poet's creative intuition is analogous to contemplative intuition.[5]

Underhill is also a spiritual guide for today through her openness to and knowledge of the mystical literature of Eastern religions and of non-Western churches. She helped Rabindranath Tagore translate one hundred poems of Kabir, the fifteenth-century Hindu mystical poet of Mohammedan birth (*Kabir*, xxiii).

Underhill's insight enabled her to distinguish mystics like Teresa, drawn to the personal mystery of God, from others like Plotinus, who prefer impersonal symbols for God derived from space and the unknown. The greatest mystics like John of Ruysbroeck experience both the intimate and infinite depths of God.[6] In "The Future of Mysticism," 1918, Underhill described mysticism as both an experience and an intuition of the Spirit. Her practical mysticism, spiritual development for the average person, offers vision and discipline to those who recognize and activate the spiritual element in their lives. This can lead to the practice of the presence of God by steady contemplation, a reordering of desires, and loving service.[7]

In "The Essentials of Mysticism," 1920, the first among several essentials is the clear conviction of a living God as the primary interest of consciousness, and of belief in a personal self capable of communion with this God. Behind this communion is the sense of a double movement, divine self-giving and human self-giving. This can be found among Christian mystics and among Neoplatonists, Hindus, and Sufis, since all are given intuitive contact with ultimate reality (*Essentials*, 3, 4, 8-23).

In "The Mystic and the Corporate Life," Underhill explored the interdependence of the church and mystical life (*Essentials*, 25-43). In "The Mysticism of Plotinus," the core of mysticism is its need for a self-giving response to the transcendent while responding to the social side of religion (*Essentials*, 130-31). "The Authority of Personal Religious Experience," 1925, discussed criteria for assessing the authenticity of an individual religious experience: its conviction about God, its emergence from corporate experience, its transforming power, and its loving impulse to selfless action (EU-Greene 119-31).

In *The Mystics of the Church*, 1925, Underhill called mysticism the "direct intuition or experience of God" and the mystic one whose life and religion are based on first-hand personal knowledge. The mystics are "the eyes of the Body of Christ," keeping the prophetic element of religion alive and showing the place of mystical spirituality in the corporate life of the church: prayer informs action. Far from being spiritual freaks, the mystics are the greatest teachers of prayer and mediate a special knowledge of God. Mysticism is neither a theory nor a name for religious sensations, but a life involving growth and creativity (*Mystics*, 9–25).

In 1926, Underhill described mysticism in its widest sense as "the reaching out of the soul to contact with those eternal realities which are the subject matter of religion" (*House*, 107). Mystical life is "the complete life of love and prayer which transmutes those objects of belief into living realities" (*House*, 107). In *Man and the Supernatural*, 1927, mystics are those "who insist that they know for certain the presence and activity of that which they call the love of God" (*Man*, 21). Adoration is the heart of religion (*Man*, 58, 198, 215).

All of this gave Underhill a sense of the mystery and unity of religious experience through her knowledge of mysticism. She wrote to Maisie Spense: "If there is one thing I seem to have learned in the course of my spiritual wanderings, it is the oblique nature of all religious formulations without exception and the deep underlying unity of all supernatural experience" (*Letters*, 255). This she based on both her own experience and her interpretation of others': "Sometimes it seems that we are bathed in a living Ocean that pours into every corner of our being to cleanse, heal and refresh. Sometimes it seems that a personal energy compels, withstands, enlightens or suddenly changes us" (*Sequence*, 64). She was what she held a mystical theologian to be: "It is this loving discernment of Reality through and in prayer, this ever-expanding experience of God, which is meant by the phrase 'mystical theology' as employed by the great Christian masters of the spiritual life" (*Sequence*, 81).

Living the Spiritual Life:
Life According to the Mystic Way

Evelyn Underhill was a seasoned student who could quote copiously from the mystics. But she understood such knowledge to be valuable only insofar as it nourishes life. She focused on the record of mystical experience so that others could enter into it.

Mary, the Mother of God, was a paradigm of how to live the spiritual life.[8] In *The Mystic Way*, Jesus of Nazareth tangibly and definitively mediates that way (*Mystic Way*, 35; EU-Brame 241). Mysticism is a way of life, not a type of knowledge. It integrates our life with God and our life in the world by a life-giving surrender to the mystery of God. It is receptive, attentive, and energetic in response. The mystic way is an organic process of growth.[9]

In her work on individual mystics, she was careful to give not only the background and context of their lives and writings, but also a critical assessment of their usefulness as models for us. What she appreciated in each of them reveals something of her own interior life. She considered Jacopone da Todi among the most individual and profound of thirteenth-century mystics.[10] The value of "The Mirror of Simple Souls" is its view of freedom as the main aim of the spiritual life. What made Angela of Foligno a Franciscan mystic were the character of her penance, her passionate devotion to the cross, and the metaphysical quality of her most outstanding mystical insights. Julian of Norwich's doctrine of love is more profound than Angela's, and her doctrine of prayer avoids both the intellectualism of the Neoplatonist and the exuberance of the religious emotionalist. Thérèse of Lisieux grew up in a world of piety devoid of intellectual conflict, yet Underhill acknowledged her genius for the spiritual life.

Charles Péguy tried to restore the homey everyday faith rooted in tradition, not in rationalism.[11] Having remarked on François Malaval's blindness, she added the pun: "The homeliness of the teaching may easily blind the rest of us to its lofty character."[12]

In her editions of and introductions to the classics of English mysticism, Underhill demonstrated control of the material, a knowledge of manuscripts and printed editions, and a grasp of the authors' lives and doctrines as she assessed the contemporary usefulness of each work. In her edition of The Cloud of Unknowing, 1910, she stressed its insistence on a wholeness of experience rather than on a quietism or a spiritual limpness.[13] The chief contribution of Walter Hilton's The Scale of Perfection is its focus on the end of our journey in faith, which demands both service and adoration.[14] Her introduction to Richard Rolle's The Fire of Love called him the "English Francis" because of his romantic and passionate nature.[15]

In her biography of John of Ruysbroeck, Underhill saw his most original contribution to the history of mysticism to be the description of superessence, in which the person is freed to become God's hidden child (Ruysbroeck, 85). Her edition of three of Ruysbroeck's works made them available to English readers for the first time.[16] She called him the greatest of the Flemish mystics and emphasized "fruition" as his favorite term for the consummation of the mystical life (Adornment, xi, xxii). He was her favorite mystic (*Letters*, 122), although she relied very much on John of the Cross for his substantive doctrine of the dark night.[17]

Life according to the mystic way was for Evelyn Underhill a balanced life of surrender to the mystery of God and the acceptance of reality. It was a process of growth in faith, freedom, and fidelity to God's call. Faith was not a product of rationalism but the pattern of trust in one's personal relationship with God, which issued in adoration and service. Freedom was not self-indulgence but self-giving that sprang from the heart's desire. Fidelity was not a matter of routine behavior but the courage to live the truth of one's being.

Growth in Prayer through Self-Sacrificing Love: A Practical Mysticism

Evelyn Underhill believed in a practical mysticism based on growth in prayer through self-sacrificing love. Images and themes recurred in her spiritual writings: the centrality of love, the image of Martha and Mary, incorporation of the homey into one's experience of the transcendent, life according to the mystic way, the metaphor of God as beauty, the mystical experience of the real presence of Christ, the symbol of Mary as mother of God, and the value of redemptive suffering.[18] These themes grew stronger in her later work.[19]

She called contemplation attention to the things of the Spirit and urged the necessary link between work and prayer (*Essentials*, 95–97). In her essay "The Place of Will, Intellect and Feeling in Prayer," she noted the benefits and disadvantages of each faculty for prayer (*Essentials*, 103–15).

In her 1921 Upton Lectures on Religion delivered at Manchester College, Oxford, she maintained that religion is committed to a synthesis of the eternal and the temporal and acclaimed the universality and unity of the life of the Spirit (*Life*, 1–28). She insisted on the unity of the self, and she integrated psychology into her own worldview by treating the intimate relationship between suggestion and religious experience (*Life*, 101–2; EU-Greene 91–92).

In her 1924 retreat on "Sanctity: The Perfection of Love," she described love as utter self-giving that is interested in every detail. She grouped her meditations around love, joy, and peace, instead of faith, hope, and love. Her 1925 retreat addresses on "The End for Which We

Were Made" showed the influence of Ignatius Loyola. Praise, reverence, and service of God is the end for which we were created, since
we come from God, belong to God, and are destined for God. She knew
that Ignatius put adoration before service, and like him she advocated
surrender even in suffering (EU-Brame 47–144, 241).

In 1926, she published a book of addresses to Anglican parish priests
called *Concerning the Inner Life*, which spelled out their primary duty:
to become and to continue to be people of real prayer and loving service (*House*, 91–108). To this end, she recommended regular adoration,
spiritual reading, meditation, intercession, and self-oblation in some
definite spiritual work. While urging those in dryness to turn to some
secular interest or recreation, she affirmed that the priest's devotional
life shows its worth in work done in times of dryness and desolation.
To help parish priests integrate prayer and action, she urged them to
pray in their own churches, to pray for those they serve, and to be
available for spiritual direction, trusting that their greatest resource
is their own life of communion with God (*House*, 109–51; *Mount*,
247–82).

In a 1926 pamphlet, she described prayer as the life of adoration and
adherence to God. Intercession for her is not only asking God for things
but collaborating with God in serving others. In 1927, she observed that
conversion has more to do with a steady growth in prayer than with an
initial crisis (EU-Greene 135–43, 154).

In her 1927 retreat called "Inner Grace and Outward Sign," she spoke
of redemptive love as helping and suffering for others, a love based on
adoration, communion, and cooperation. In her 1928 retreat addresses
on "The Call of God," all of us must find our identity in God and let
ourselves be plunged into the ocean of God's love by surrender that
leads to service (EU-Brame 145–240).

In 1929, she used the metaphor of "the house of the soul" to describe
our call to become a house of prayer in the world. She wrote of a life of
surrendered love that is both world-embracing and world-renouncing
(*House*, 3–11, 23). She brought an original twist to the metaphor, emphasizing how holistic we must be, making our whole house a house of
prayer, feeling comfortable on the lowest floor as well as on the upper
floor. She wrote:

> The whole house with its manifold and graded activities must be a
> house of prayer. It does not mean keeping a Quiet Room to which
> we can retreat, with mystical pictures on the walls, and curtains

over the windows to temper the disconcerting intensity of the light; a room where we can forget the fact that there are black beetles in the kitchen, and that the range is not working very well. Once we admit any violent contrast between the upper and lower floor, the "instinctive" and "spiritual" life, or feel a reluctance to investigate the humbling realities of the basement, our life becomes less, not more, than human and our position is unsafe.[20]

Another instance of her domestic originality is found in the following observation: "The house of the soul is properly furnished; the cleaning materials are all there. The languors and difficulties of ill-health, the friction of uncongenial temperaments, the hard rubs of circumstance, can all leave us cleaner than before" (*House*, 70).

Mysticism bears practical fruit: "The goal of our spiritual growth is not some special beatitude, some peculiar condition of awareness but humble and useful cooperation with God" (*Sequence*, 62). To speak of our spiritual life is not to speak of ourselves but of God and the divine action working in union with our own (*Sequence*, 63).

In addresses given at the House of Retreat, Pleshey, in May 1932, Underhill urged freshness and creativity: "We must keep our prayer free, frank, youthful — full of confidence and full of initiative too" (*Light of Christ*, 45; *School*, 49). A retreat can deepen and renew a sense of rebirth, a sense of proportion, and a sense of one's personal relationship with God (*Light*, 102–7). Her 1936 retreat addresses summarized the fruits of the Spirit as deep delight in God, peaceful acceptance of the gifts in our life, and creaturely acceptance of our call and limitations (*Fruits*, 7–43).

In *Mixed Pasture*, 1933, Underhill described contemplation as "the art whereby we have communion with that ultimate reality,... the very life blood of religion" (*Mixed*, 1,5; cf. 7–8). She called again for the integration of the practical and the contemplative life. We must find God in our practical everyday life, work, and suffering, as well as in our prayer life.[21]

In a 1936 broadcast talk published as *The Spiritual Life*, Underhill approached the spiritual life as something other than the life of one's psyche, much less as a sort of honors course in personal religion (*Spiritual Life*, 11). She warned against an individualistic cultivation of one's own soul and insisted that the spiritual life is intensely social. She lived this conviction by doing regular volunteer work with the poor in the North Kensington slums. She saw that conflicts and difficulties arise from our separation of life's spiritual and practical aspects. She saw the spiritual life as God's affair produced by the divine attraction and our self-forgetful response to it.[22] Her horizon is global: "The meaning of our life is bound up with the meaning of the universe" (*Spiritual Life*, 19, 37).

She also discussed the spiritual life as cooperation with God and the Lord's Prayer as "a total concentration on the total interests of God, which must be expressed in action" (*Spiritual Life*, 77). Implications of this attitude include an acceptance of the interconnectedness of politics and spirituality, willingness to serve in difficult circumstances and to suffer for others in painful self-giving, tranquillity, gentleness in the ups and downs of daily life, and openness to secret transformation, including struggle, effort, and sacrifice. For her, the important task is to maintain ongoing correlation between the inner and the outer (*Spiritual Life*, 81, 86–98).

In *Abba*, 1940, Underhill described prayer as the substance of eternal life and adoration as the necessary preparation for action (*Abba*, 1, 22). Growth in prayer comes about in the school of love (*School*, 49; *Light*, 46). The implication is obvious: "Those who complain that they make no progress in the life of prayer because they 'cannot meditate' should examine, not their capacity for meditation, but their capacity for suffering and love" (*School*, 54).

Underhill's reverence for the Spirit and for our openness to the Spirit led her to write: "The Spirit is one of those guests for whom space must be made; whose presence makes a difference for the whole house, and not merely to the spare room" (*School*, 85). She accepted weakness as a form of openness to the Spirit (*School*, 88; *Light*, 49).

In *The Mount of Purification*, 1931 retreat addresses, Underhill called prayer "fundamental spiritual activity," and stated that "humble surrender, not constant fervor, is the best index of the soul's good-will" (*Mount*, 161, 166). Steeped in mystical literature, she proposed her own five divisions of prayer: vocal prayer, meditation, the prayer of immediate acts, the prayer of simplicity, and the prayer of quiet (*Mount*, 167–77).

In her view, intercession is not only a petition but a work involving self-surrender to God. She distrusted an individualistic, subjective approach to prayer, "a self-cultivating, self-exploring job." Our prayer is the prayer of living members of the church. Following the French school of spirituality, she described the three movements of the life of prayer as adoration, communion, and cooperation with God (*Mount*, 185, 301–2).

An attitude of heart that she often urged in her letters was self-surrender: "Self-surrender, an entire willingness to live in the dark, in pain, anything — this is the real secret."[23] Such surrender was part of her balance between life with God and life in the world. It includes the willingness to suffer, confidence, and grateful acceptance of the divine presence (*Letters*, 129, 153, 168, 174, 194, 223).

But another attitude of heart is a balanced view toward life. One example can be found in this letter:

> Develop and expand the wholesome, natural and intellectual interests of your life — don't allow yourself to concentrate on the religious side only.... Get the necessary variety and refreshment without which religious intensity soon becomes stale. (*Letters*, 178)

In a letter five years later, she gave this wise counsel:

> Early bed, novels, the flicks and so on are all good and help to minimize the nervous strain. Do not be too ferocious in your exercises in detachment at the moment, and try not to be discouraged, though I know this is hard. Your grief at God's absence is the best of all proofs of your love. (*Letters*, 224–25)

Evelyn Underhill is a woman of faith for our times. She served as a spiritual guide for laypeople urging the integration of the sacred and the secular. As a laywoman herself, she knew what it was to juggle the demands of family and home with a commitment to prayer, research, writing, and community worship. In a letter she wrote: "Bring your whole situation *en bloc* into your Godward life. Knock down the partition between living-room and oratory, even if it does mean tobacco smoke and incense get a bit mixed up" (*Letters*, 217). In a letter to a friend, she wrote with prudence and a respect for the secular dimension of spirituality:

> Take *special* pains now to keep up fully or develop some definite nonreligious interest, e.g., your music. Work at it, consider it an obligation to do so. It is most necessary to your spiritual health; and you will very soon find that it has a steadying effect. "Good works" won't do — it must be something you really like for its own sake.... Hot milk and a thoroughly foolish novel are better things for you to go to bed on just now than St. Teresa. (*Letters*, 313)

Growth in prayer comes from the practical mysticism of daily loving. It entails the gift of self to others and to God in union with Christ.

Cultivation of the Spirit of Worship: Adoration in Daily Life

We cultivate the spirit of adoration by learning to worship not only on Sundays but daily. In her second major work, *Worship*, 1937, Underhill called worship the response of the creature to the eternal and an acknowledgment of transcendence.[24] She showed Christian worship in its various expressions: the nun or monk rising to recite the Divine Office in the night, the Quaker waiting silently for the Spirit, the ritualist preparing a complex ceremonial, and "the old woman content to boil her potatoes in the same sacred intention" (*Worship*, 68). Christian worship cannot be divorced from the sanctification of life (*Worship*, 78–79). Like Christianity, other sects and religions possess positive elements of worship, that is, the movement of adoration, dependence, and self-offering, which outweigh the possible negative elements of worship, such as routine, rigidity, and formalism (*Worship*, xii, 11).

Underhill systematically examined worship in various religious traditions. She explored the influence of the Jewish temple and synagogue on Christian worship. In her opinion, Catholic worship is theocentric, incarnational, sacrificial, social, and organic. She dwelt on the icon in Orthodox worship and on the "prayer of the heart," most familiar as the Jesus-prayer. Among the Reformed churches, she recognized the centrality of the proclamation of the Word of God, while the "priesthood of all believers" governed free church worship, finding its extreme in the Quaker preference for spontaneous worship and pure inwardness. She held that the Anglican cult combined a Catholic sacramental and corporate ideal of Christian worship with the Protestant biblical and individual ideal (*Worship*, 193–253, 262–338).

She sought a spirit of worship in education. She reminded teachers to cultivate a sense of the sacred and of the beautiful so as to help others interpret the world and to learn to look with the eyes of adoration. Those who see life with admiration and reverence are the best guides for living. The essential elements of this spirit of worship are faith, hope, and love. Worship involves a selfless, total devotion to the great designs of creation (*Mount*, 314–33).

Evelyn Underhill cultivated such a spirit and invited others to do so. This was not a religiosity threatened by scientific advances, but rather a perspective that viewed life in the context of eternity.

Renewed Commitment to the Church: Incarnational Unity

The fact that Evelyn Underhill ended her life with a renewed commitment to the church is all the more remarkable when one recalls her early ambivalence about membership in a religious institution. The intellectual barriers to becoming a Roman Catholic in 1907 did not lead her immediately to Anglicanism. She gradually stopped going to Mass and relied on her own individual religious experience. But by 1918, she concluded that personal religion needs an institutional framework. In 1920, she became a member of a confraternity of Christians who prayed for one another. By 1921, she seemed to be fully in the Anglican communion (EU-Greene, 5–8).

In "Christian Fellowship," 1924, she asserted that in healthy religious groups, the building of community is secondary to developing a personal relationship with God and that the secret of fellowship is congruence of an aim that transcends the members (EU-Greene, 105–7). In her 1925 article "Our Two-Fold Relation to Reality," Underhill saw the defects in religious institutions but also their capacity to train people for God by transmitting the wisdom of tradition (EU-Greene, 170).

She summarized the contributions and limitations of a church for its members, emphasizing its conservation and development of tradition. Life lived fully incorporates contemplation, discipline, and service. Spirituality must not be a merely self-regarding pastime but an education for action.[25]

She increasingly saw the need for both organized and personal religion, for corporate worship as well as for private adoration (*Man*, 77, 83, 215). Hence she could criticize modernism for its rejection of religious institutions in favor of the authority of personal religious experience (*Man*, 88).

Her metaphors for the church are original: an organism, not a mere crowd of souls, a reality grounded in God, not a Spiritual Rotary Club; an organ of the Spirit, not a devotional guild (*School*, 92, 100, 104). She preferred regular communal worship to the solitary reading of esoteric spiritual books.[26]

As to the ministry of women, she made it clear that she opposed women's ordination for many reasons, chiefly that such a break with tradition needed the consent of the whole church (*Mixed*, 113). Her ideals of women's ministry included loving abandonment to God and Christ, informality and freedom, a prophetic way of serving God and people, and a quietness and hiddenness about one's best work. She foresaw women in many new and important kinds of ministry. Her guideline was that usefulness depends on constant cooperation with God (*Mixed*, 113-18, 120-21). Even though many women do not agree with her position on women's ordination, they can still look to her as a spiritual guide challenging them to deepen and develop attitudes of heart that would characterize their own ordained ministry.

The influence of Baron von Hügel on Evelyn Underhill was enormous.[27] Between 1921 and his death in 1925, she moved from idealism to critical realism, from a disembodied mysticism to an incarnational spirituality of finding God in the world, and from a theocentric orientation to a Christocentric devotion to people (EU-Greene, 9). Much of her advice to others came from his advice to her: to develop some nonreligious interests, to get involved with the poor, and to participate in the corporate life and worship of the church.[28] He also used the word "homely," which can be rendered "homey."[29]

Von Hügel supported Underhill's renewed commitment to traditional, institutional, and sacramental religion.[30] He understood her difficulty with the virgin birth, the bodily resurrection of Jesus, and the Johannine miracles, and helped her interpret these happenings in faith but also in the light of critical reason.[31] He confirmed that she remain an Anglican since God had not called her decisively to do otherwise (*Letters*, 196). Perhaps his greatest gift was as mediator and facilitator of her personal relationship with Christ.[32]

Her sense of the church was ecumenical. She participated in the movement for reconciliation between Orthodox and Anglicans. And she became part of another movement for the reunion of churches that made an annual forty-day crusade of prayer.[33] Her letters consistently promoted church unity (*Letters*, 257-58, 285).

Underhill came to see the struggle for peace as part of her Christian commitment and sense of church. In 1915, she published two articles condoning war as a necessary evil and urging patriotic support.[34] But later, in light of her experience of the violence and horror of World War I, she became a pacifist. Just before World War II, she joined the Anglican Peace Fellowship and wrote a pamphlet called *The Church and War*, which warned against the church acquiescing in war, although she believed in legitimate police action, and invited communicant Christians to join the Anglican Peace Fellowship (Cropper, 214-15). For the Fellowship of Reconciliation, another pacifist group, she wrote a *Meditation of Peace*, in which she called the true pacifist a redeemer who is self-offered for the peace of the world.[35] Her letters from 1937 on speak of pacifism and her commitment to it.[36]

Underhill's renewed commitment to the church was developmental. In its growing focus on incarnational unity, it gradually came to include institutional, ecumenical, and pacifist dimensions.

Conclusion

Evelyn Underhill's unitive knowledge of mysticism was based on a combination of her interpretation of others' religious experience and her personal and corporate experience of God. Living the spiritual life meant living according to the mystic way, which includes not only prolonged prayer but also a life of service. She advocated a practical mysticism that gauged growth in prayer by the quality of self-sacrificing love. She cultivated the spirit of worship by seeing God in homey details. Her renewed commitment to the church was based on a balance of prayer, service, and community.

Experience was her point of departure. Poor health gave her ample opportunity to undergo purification at many levels. She let her experience be her guide in dealing with others, warning them to balance prayer and spiritual reading with relaxation and the cultivation of nonreligious interests. Unable to approach mysticism in an abstract way, she emphasized points by giving examples from the lives and writings of the mystics. Her work with the poor raised her consciousness about their concerns and gave her courage to speak out on social issues and to be in the vanguard of those whose spirituality includes social justice.[37] As Richard Woods has observed, she contributed significantly to the contemporary philosophical understanding of mysticism and laid foundations for further studies in the comparative study of religion.[38]

According to Charles Williams, "The proof of her calling — or, at least, the value of it — was in her motherhood of souls" (*Letters*, 26). For him, Underhill's vocation was to be not so much a guide as a light illuminating and shining (*Letters*, 44).

Margaret Cropper described Underhill aptly as a "mediator of God's

reality" (Cropper, 102). She wrote of Underhill's "special power of making the things of the Spirit seem both tremendous and homely, and
curiously attractive" (Cropper, 138).

One can argue that there were two Evelyns, the joyous discoverer of
the eternal and the older religious leader who taught many the meaning
of Christian living.[39] But one can also observe that Christianity integrated these facets of her personality, freeing her to develop a personal
relationship with Christ and a deep respect for the wisdom of other
world religions.

Hers was not so much a mysticism of visions as a practical mysticism
of daily love. Like all of us, she experienced loneliness as well as love,
disappointment as well as enthusiasm, the ingratitude of others as well
as their support. Karl Rahner has taken the same view in a phrase that
encapsulates the meaning of Underhill's life and work: "a mysticism of
everyday faith."[40] This mysticism is based on a conviction of the unity
of the love of God and the love of neighbor.[41] It is a self-emptying that, as
Rahner perceives, is not "accomplished by practicing pure inwardness,
but by the real activity which is called humility, service, love of our
neighbor, the cross and death."[42] It holds that the experience of the
mystics is different not in kind but only in degree from the ordinary
Christian life of faith, hope, and love. Mysticism as an experience of
transcendence and of radical faith is available to everyone.[43] It is in this
sense of experiencing God in daily life, of being open to the mystery of
transcendence in the rhythm of our homey joys and sorrows, our hopes
and fears, that we can agree with Karl Rahner's prophecy: "The devout
Christian of the future will either be a 'mystic,' one who has 'experienced'
something, or will cease to be anything at all."[44]

Thus, while Underhill studied mysticism in terms of its secondary
phenomena of visions, locutions, and ecstasies, she lived and taught a
mysticism of everyday faith, a mysticism that loves God by loving our
neighbor, a practical mysticism based on discovering and revealing the
transcendent in the homey. Dana Greene calls her an artist of the infinite
life, "one who knew its forms and colors, who described its expressions
over thousands of pages."[45] I call her a pathfinder for our way to God
since she respected each one's uniqueness and responded accordingly
with her insights and advice.

Evelyn Underhill is a spiritual guide for today. She lived a spirituality that is incarnational, holistic, ecumenical, political, and global. She
was comfortable in the world of the homey and in the world of the transcendent. She took a keen interest in the details of others' lives and had

a genius for friendship.[46] She insisted on a balance between times of leisure and times of prayer. To those under stress or strain wanting to pray, she urged beginning first with the relaxation of their bodies and minds.

Her respect for her own and others' religious experience can inspire us to cherish the touch of God in our lives. Her return to organized religion despite its limitations can challenge the disenchanted. Her recognition of the transcendent in the homey can strengthen our vision of faith. She witnessed to a remarkable integrity, pursuing the scholarly study of mysticism and a serious life of prayer despite a lack of support from her husband and parents. The care with which she prepared and preached a retreat is a model for those engaged in retreat work. Her spiritual advice, so full of common sense and earthy examples, rings true in our day. Uncluttered by technique, she concentrated not on teaching ways of praying but on helping people be open to the mystery of God. Her spiritual leadership in the church pioneered the way for other Anglican women to serve the church in meaningful ways.

Her pacifism was rooted in her living of gospel values. Her pacifist stance opened up socio-political implications of her love of neighbor. Her commitment to her parents, husband, friends, and the poor led her to world concerns for peace and justice.

She combined a life of scholarly research and prayer with marriage. She lived as a liberated woman balancing her own career of writing and her ministry of spiritual direction with her family and social commitments. To use her own metaphor, she was as comfortable in the basement of the "house of her soul" as on the top floor.

She made an invaluable contribution to scholarship. The fact that she herself led a committed prayer life gives her scholarly contribution to mysticism a depth and authenticity. Her familiarity with the mystics validates her reliability as a spiritual guide steeped in the Christian tradition. Her openness to other Protestant denominations and other world religions shows a conviction of the universal possibility of salvation. The breadth of her vision inspires us to stay in touch with the signs of the times.

Disenchanted by institutional faith and then renewed in its meaning, she learned the interdependence of personal and communal faith. As a married, childless laywoman, she sought and found union with God in the homey details of everyday life. A self-educated theologian, she was one of the few women of her day who saw spirituality and theology as integral to the full Christian life. Versed in Jewish, Hindu, and Orthodox mysticism, she engaged in ecumenical and interfaith dialogue. During World War II, she championed a cause that is uppermost in our times, the need for peacemaking. Through retreats and spiritual direction, she mediated God's forgiving nearness.

READINGS

The two classics of Evelyn Underhill's scholarly work are *Mysticism: A Study of the Nature and Development of Man's Spiritual Consciousness* (New York: E. P. Dutton & Co., 1961), and *Worship* (San Francisco: Harper and Bros., 1937).

Recent editions of Evelyn Underhill's works are making her writings accessible and confirming the renewed interest in her as a spiritual guide for today, for example, *The House of the Soul and Concerning the Inner Life* (Minneapolis: Seabury, 1984), and *The Life of the Spirit and the Life of Today* (San Francisco: Harper & Row, 1986). Charles Williams' collection of *The Letters of Evelyn Underhill* (Westminster, Md.: Christian Classics, 1989) gives an excellent introduction to Evelyn Underhill's personal life and capacity to give spiritual counsel. Grace Adolphsen Brame's valuable edition of four previously unknown and unpublished retreats that Evelyn Underhill presented in the 1920s, called *The Ways of the Spirit* (New York: Crossroad, 1990), makes these retreats available. Brame had to decipher the script and the sometimes cryptically written thought of original handwritten material. Christopher Armstrong's *Evelyn Underhill: An Introduction to Her Life and Writing* (Grand Rapids, Mich.: Eerdmans, 1975) gives a helpful overview.

Dana Greene has made two very significant contributions. One is her collection of hitherto uncollected essays by Underhill called *Evelyn Underhill: Modern Guide to the Ancient Quest for the Holy* (Albany, N.Y.: State University of New York Press, 1988), which contains an interpretive introduction and a comprehensive bibliography. The other is her authoritative biography of Underhill entitled *Evelyn Underhill: Artist of the Infinite Life* (New York: Crossroad, 1990).

2
DOROTHY DAY

(1897–1980)

Peacemaker in Our Nuclear Age

DOROTHY DAY'S life was a unity composed of love of neighbor and love of God. The long loneliness and hunger for God that marked her life were transformed into a community of shared faith and service to the poor. Her quest for the meaning and purpose of life became her search for a community of praise, for a religion based on a faith active in deeds of love.

Her ability to relate to people was lived through the power of the Spirit in the service of mission, the simple mission of giving bread to the hungry and shelter to the homeless. In this way, she reflected Christ's love for those who are poor. A passion for justice also shaped her life, leading her to choose a pacifist stance and voluntary poverty. Her career in journalism was transformed into the ministry we call today the Catholic Worker movement.

Day wrote as a woman of faith and developed her views on women to include not only woman as community-maker but also woman as builder of a better world. She herself knew the security of living in a happy family, the happiness of being a friend, the pleasure of being a lover, and the joy of giving herself to others. Yet she also knew the sadness of separation, the sorrow of unrequited love, and the cost of discipleship. In the narrative mode of storytelling, she interspersed her personal reminiscences with facts about the socio-political situations of her day.

Her life, work, and writings call us to conversion. In this world of technology, what does praise have to say to us? How can community life invite us out of the individualism endemic to North America? In a world in which more is considered better, can we take time to hear the cry of the poor? In a violent world full of drugs and bombs, is pacifism a realistic option? In the midst of despair and loneliness, are we willing to bond together to build a better world?

This chapter explores five attitudes of heart that qualify Dorothy Day as a peacemaker and spiritual guide in our nuclear age: praise, personal love, passion for justice, peacemaking, and commitment to the struggle of being a woman of faith.

Praise: Religion and Faith

Dorothy Day's conversion to Catholicism sprang from her need for a community of praise, a group of people with whom she could worship God. When her daughter was born, Day became a Catholic in order to worship and thank God in the company of others, to express her faith as a member of the body of Christ. In her own childhood, she was inspired by religion, reading the psalms, the New Testament, John Wesley's sermons, and the hymns from the Episcopalian hymnal (*Loneliness*, 10).

In her university years, however, strongly influenced by Karl Marx, she scorned religion as an opiate for the people and concentrated on her love for the masses (*Loneliness*, 19–46). When she moved to New York and worked for a Socialist daily paper, she was appalled by the sight of homeless and unemployed men on the streets (*Loneliness*, 51).

In jail for protesting at the White House against political arrests, she asked for a Bible and rediscovered her love for the psalms. Not wanting to acknowledge her need for God in defeat and sorrow, she pretended she was reading for literary enjoyment: "I prayed and did not know that I prayed" (*Loneliness*, 81). Returning to New York, she made it a habit to go to an early morning Mass in order to be in the atmosphere of praise, of people taking time to pray together in a sacred space: "People have so great a need to reverence, to worship, to adore; it is a psychological necessity of human nature that must be taken into account" (*Loneliness*, 84). She reflected that she was not yet conscious of praying (*Loneliness*, 85).

Dorothy shared a house with Forster Batterham on the beach in Staten Island and read the Bible and the *Imitation of Christ*, a fifteenth-century spiritual treatise with a strong ascetical bent. She began consciously to pray more, praying with open-eyed gratitude at sunset on the beach, listening to waves and seagulls and the Angelus bell. She prayed the rosary walking to the village for mail, said the *Te*

Deum on the beach, talked to Mary, the Mother of God, as she worked about the house, and went to Mass on Sunday mornings. She realized that she was praying not because she was in grief or despair, not because she needed consolation, but rather because she was happy and wanted to thank God. She became pregnant, thrilled by the mystery of her pregnancy. After the birth of her child, she felt the need to adore (*Loneliness*, 114–39).

She wanted to join the Catholic Church as a community of praise, but knew it would mean giving up her common-law husband, Forster, and felt she had to choose between him and God. She had Tamar Teresa baptized, and finally she decided to be baptized herself although this would mean the inevitable separation from the man she loved. From the vantage point of post-Vatican II, one wonders if so violent a wrenching would have been necessary today.[1]

With the help of Peter Maurin, another committed Christian, Dorothy founded what came to be called the Catholic Worker movement. In May 1933, in New York City, they began publishing a newspaper called the *Catholic Worker*, selling it at one cent a copy.

Peter's program of action included houses of hospitality, round-table discussions, and farming communes. Together they converted some farm houses into retreat houses so working people could get away to pray and relax. They had "worker retreats" and days of recollection. Sometimes they would invite a priest to talk to them about the love of God and abandonment to divine providence, while workers came and went, ate and slept. At other times, they went to a convent where they prayed and fasted.

Dorothy realized that it was not only for others that she made these retreats, but for her own nourishment (*Loneliness*, 198, 243–63). In 1941 and 1943, she made week-long retreats with John Hugo, a diocesan priest in Pittsburgh, based on retreat notes by Onesimus Lacouture, a French Canadian priest from Montreal. These retreats brought her to new levels in her relationship with God. She was drawn to take a leave of absence for prolonged prayer and visits with her daughter and mother from September 1943 until March 1944 when Tamar was married (*Day*, 361).

Her writings are sprinkled with references to and quotations from the Judeo-Christian Scriptures, the Christian mystics, the saints, and Catholic authors of both sacred and secular literature. She had great devotion to St. Joseph as the patron of families.[2] She was often inspired by Teresa of Avila, who is clearly one of her own spiritual guides.[3] And she was drawn to the "little way" of Thérèse of Lisieux, who was so much like the rest of us in her ordinariness.[4]

She found that she was nourished by daily Mass, the Office, meditation, spiritual reading, the rosary, Benediction, and days of recollection. She was also helped by other means to contemplative prayer, like a symphony on the radio, the goodness of people, natural beauty, and novels by Dostoevsky and Tolstoy.[5] Such prayer springs from the heart rather than being based on the recitation of vocal prayers. She combined the devotional aspect of her spirituality with her liberationist radicalism, and included in the lists of the dead for whom she prayed martyrs of the labor movement, miners, Memorial Day massacre victims, and people tortured and lynched (*Sixties*, 197). Day had a strong sense of corporateness in the body of Christ, of identification with the other members of the body of Christ. In particular, she had a strong sense of suffering with Christ; she identified with him as a member of his body (*Union*, 7, 11, 16). At the same time, she had a strong sense of social sin.

Her spirituality was based on trying to encounter Christ in daily life.[6] It was incarnational and, in particular, centered on the Eucharist, connecting the material with the spiritual (*Union*, 11–12).

Her attraction for worship and thanksgiving was her call to prayer. This need to praise underlay the search that had led her to become a Roman Catholic. She needed to make peace with God, the God of her happiness who had given her new life.

Personal Love: *Eros* and *Agape*

Dorothy Day had a tremendous capacity for love. In her lifetime, she experienced different kinds of loving relationships: family life, friendship, romance, a common-law marriage, motherhood, celibacy, and service to the poor. She serves as a spiritual guide for us in her openness to human intimacy.

When Dorothy was fourteen, she began to love deeply her new baby brother, John, rocking him to sleep, singing hymns, and feeding him his bottle. At the same time, she "fell in love" with the musician who led the band in Lincoln Park for the concerts (*Loneliness*, 30–33). Dorothy's capacity for friendship with women was expressed in her relationship with Rayna Simons, a Jewish student at the University of Illinois. Rayna died a sudden tragic death as a communist in Moscow. Dorothy saw her as "an anonymous Christian," or, if you will, an anonymous graced one:

"When I think of Rayna, I think of Mauriac's statement in his life of Christ that those who serve the cause of the masses, the poor, working for truth and justice, have worked for Christ even while denying Him."[7]

While working as a nurse at a Brooklyn hospital, Day fell in love with Lionel Moise, a newspaperman, and began living with him in November 1918, becoming pregnant the following spring. Knowing Moise would desert her if she had a child, she had an abortion in September 1919, and then learned he had left her. During their affair, she apparently attempted suicide. Months later, she married Barkeley Tobey and went to Europe. But after only one year of this stormy marriage, she returned to the United States and divorced Tobey. She then lived in Chicago for two years, hoping to resume her relationship with Moise, but he was not interested, and in the fall of 1923 she moved to New Orleans. Her autobiographical novel, *The Eleventh Virgin*, which concludes with her abortion and abandonment by Moise, was published in 1924.[8]

She moved back to New York and met another man with whom she lived and learned about love: "The man I loved, with whom I entered into a common-law marriage, was an anarchist, an Englishman by descent, and a biologist" (*Loneliness*, 113). Thus she described Forster Batter-ham with whom she lived in a beach house on Staten Island, New York. The only barrier between them was religion. Yet it was he who mediated God to her: "I have always felt that it was life with him that brought me natural happiness, that brought me to God. His ardent love of creation brought me to the Creator of all things" (*Loneliness*, 134). She realized that love between a woman and a man was not incompatible with love of God. She was grateful for *eros*, for sexual love and so for life. She felt they were co-creators with God of the baby she bore, Tamar Teresa. But he had no use for God or religion and could not support her having their baby baptized and becoming a Catholic herself. So she finally separated from him.

With Peter Maurin, she began to live community life that was at the service of poor and destitute people. It seems she never became romantically involved with him; theirs was a strong friendship and collaboration based on faith, respect, affection, and a common love for the poor. She chose celibacy for the sake of availability to God and to others. Even in the midst of her burgeoning ministry, however, she felt keenly the loss of physical intimacy that her celibate state imposed (*Loneliness*, 236).

In her reflections on the growth of the Catholic Worker houses of hospitality, she wrote of finding the love of God through loving our neighbor, finding the one whom our heart loves in the poor. Day wrote of reform coming through the love of God that leads us to love each other, reminding us that the love of God and the love of neighbor must go hand in hand and that this one love is a lifelong task. She chose in faith not to dwell on her own weakness but to see Christ in others more clearly.[9]

Dorothy Day knew of the human need to make peace. She experienced community as the social answer to the long loneliness. She believed that we show our love for God by living, working, sharing together, by loving our neighbor, and by living close to God. We know God and each other in the breaking of bread where we are not alone. Her commitment to *agape*, to table fellowship, is counter-cultural in our nuclear age, which advocates individualism, materialism, and militarism. For Dorothy Day, power, prestige, and fame are superseded by powerlessness, humility, and the following of Christ poor.

Passion for Justice: Christ's Love for the Poor

Dorothy Day's love of the poor, the worker, and the unemployed inspired her "passion for justice."[10] She was originally influenced by reading social novels of Russians and of Americans such as Upton Sinclair and Jack London. As a New York journalist writing for a socialist paper, she covered protests and strikes, most of which grew out of some human misery, such as a death in a family from fire, starvation, or eviction (*Loneliness*, 61). Once, while visiting a prostitute who had made a suicide attempt, Day was arrested on the charge of prostitution. In jail, she felt shame and self-contempt. It was for her an experience of solidarity with these poor. "I was sharing, as I never had before, the life of the poorest of the poor, the guilty, the dispossessed" (*Loneliness*, 104). A friend of hers arranged for her release and the case was dismissed (*Loneliness*, 105).

She went to Washington to report on the Hunger March for *Commonweal* and the Farmers Convention for *America*, both Catholic journals. She recalled how these farmworkers were Christ's poor with whom he had identified and who had been betrayed by Christianity (*House*, xiii). After the demonstration, she visited the National Shrine at Catholic University on the feast of the Immaculate Conception, where she prayed that she could use the talents she had been given for her fellow workers, for poor people: "And when I returned to New York, I found Peter Maurin — Peter the French peasant" (*Loneliness*, 166).

Peter began to educate her in the history of the church, to teach her Catholic philosophy, and to form her to see Christ in others. Peter advocated voluntary poverty, doing without luxuries in order to enable people to buy the necessities. In her efforts to work for justice in faith, she was pelted with rotten eggs and branded as a slum landlady. She was convinced that the vocation of the *Catholic Worker* was to reach the person in the street, to convey Catholic social teaching as a basis for social reconstruction (*Loneliness*, 170–88, 195; *Sixties*, 21, 54, 148).

Day's attitude toward poor and destitute people was transformed by faith. Early in her life, she had felt a love for these people, a natural desire to hear and respond to the cry of the poor. Later in her life, she was also drawn to love them in faith, to love them as Christ loves them, to love them with his love: "We felt a respect for the poor and destitute as those nearest to God, as those chosen by Christ for His compassion" (*Loneliness*, 204). Grace built on nature. She began to read the gospel through the eyes of the workers she served, noticing that Jesus made up parables about the migrant worker and the proletariat, speaking of the living wage that those who came at the eleventh hour received (*Loneliness*, 205). Her underlying conviction was that "we must and will find Christ in each and every man, when we look on them as brothers" (*Loneliness*, 216). Yet it was clear that even with a good social order, there would always be the lame, the blind, and the poor whom Christ loves. She saw Christ in the hungry and unemployed people in the Catholic Worker breadline (*House*, 239–59).

The stand she took to defend the dignity and rights of workers to strike was influenced by her father's sense of social justice instilled in her as a child. It was based on the fact that human beings are not to be treated as chattels but as temples of the Holy Spirit and co-creators with God. Their labor is not a commodity to be bought and sold but rather a discipline and a vocation. She envisioned laborers becoming partners and sharers in responsibility and in the ownership of private property (*House*, 142–49, 226–27).

A member of many communist affiliate organizations but never a "signed up" member of the Communist Party, she decided in later years that communism was a false doctrine brought about by the failure of Christians. She was against its atheistic stance, its support of violent revolution, and its denial of the natural right of private property. She saw in communists a love of friends but not a love of enemies. She felt they lacked any sense of connectedness among people under God. Her attraction to Marxism was due to its recognition of the dignity of the person and of labor. Her disillusionment with communism was for its dictatorship of the propertyless, maintained by violence. She believed that real communism can be achieved only through world community (*Union*, 146–51). She perceived that communists could be anonymous Christians, or anonymous graced ones: "If the Chinese and the Cubans are working for justice, and a better life for the masses, are they not also working for Christ, though they do not know him?" (*Sixties*, 237).

In the 1930s, Dorothy was actively involved in the union movement, justice and equality for black people, and pacifism. In the 1960s, she became actively involved in the social issues of America about which she wrote, such as Castro's violent revolution in Cuba, Martin Luther King's nonviolent struggle for justice for black people, the peace movement, and César Chávez's nonviolent leadership in the California grape boycott.[11] She was keenly aware of our need for conversion, for a revolution of the heart whereby we take the lowest place, wash the feet of others, and love others with that passion for justice that leads to the Cross.[12] Dorothy dreamt of the day when workers would take over the means of production to start to build that kind of society where each received according to need and worked according to ability (*Loneliness*, 85).

Peacemaking: Poverty and Pacifism

Dorothy Day was a peacemaker, willing to be poor in order to be a pacifist. She believed that the poverty of spirit that characterizes abandonment to divine providence is inseparable from material poverty. She admitted that poverty was her vocation (*Sixties*, 30). Choosing to live simply was, for her, choosing to make peace.

She was cheered by the poverty of the Catholic Worker houses that depend on voluntary contributions to provide food and money to pay their bills. She did not, however, believe in destitution, and was always careful to make that distinction. She believed that an acceptance of "decent poverty" is the way to improve the social order.[13] For her, the love of neighbor implied voluntary poverty, involving regional living, that is, not eating foods grown in a region other than our own. Poverty also meant having a bare minimum of clothes and being sure that they have been made under decent working conditions (*Pilgrimage*, 166–68). She made it clear that she connected voluntary poverty with pacifism:

All our talks about peace and the weapons of the spirit are meaningless unless we try in every way to embrace *voluntary poverty* and not work in any position, any job, that contributes to war, not to take any job whose pay comes from the fear of war, of the atom bomb. (*Pilgrimage*, 82-83)

The theme of abandonment to divine providence recurs in her writings.[14] In her book on Thérèse of Lisieux, a Christian who strongly advocated this attitude of heart, Day claims that in the face of the threat of nuclear disaster, Thérèse is releasing a spiritual force upon the universe to counteract that fear: "We know that one impulse of grace is of infinitely more power than a cobalt bomb. Thérèse has said, 'All is grace.'"[15]

She is a spiritual guide for us in her description of interior and personal poverty:

One can only judge the practice of poverty in others by the generosity they evidence in sharing not only their material goods, but their physical, mental and spiritual wealth, and the generosity they evidence in giving their time, that most precious possession in this too short life. (*Sixties*, 267)

As part of her call to peacemaking, Dorothy Day stood strongly and consistently in favor of pacifism. She wrote in the *Catholic Worker* about race war, class war, the Spanish civil war, World War II, and the Korean War, believing that moral force can be substituted for coercion in an effort to avoid violence (*Loneliness*, 264, 270-71). In spite of the Depression, she continued to be radical, consistent, and risk-taking in her pacifism. During World War II, she printed a column in the *Catholic Worker* encouraging men not to register for the draft (*Loaves*, 60).

She advocated sit-down strikes as a form of nonviolent resistance (*House*, 197). After having visited a group of striking auto workers, she became more convinced than ever of the need for organization, a long-range program of action, and an educational orientation based on a philosophy of labor underlying cooperatives and credit unions (*House*, 199). Picketing against housing discrimination and protesting the draft were for her works of mercy (*Pilgrimage*, 130). Picket lines, sit-ins, and the passing out of handbills, were acts of faith, hope, and charity (*Sixties*, 172).

She maintained that the Catholic Worker was distinguished from other movements by its attitudes toward our industrial civilization, the machine, and war. She saw the importance of people being fed, but also employed, in order to be co-creators with God. She supported "distributism," which advocated the right and responsibility of private property, and opposed machine technology, capitalism, and urban life. In fact, she claimed that the advocacy of pacifism and distributism distinguished the Catholic Worker movement from many other forms of the lay apostolate (*Pilgrimage*, 80–82). She criticized capitalism for the ways it provides arms and supplies for war.

The Catholic Worker movement was heavily influenced by the Christian personalism of Emmanuel Mounier and Jacques Maritain, twentieth-century French philosophers who insisted on the primacy of Christian love and denounced the dehumanizing aspects of nationalism and capitalism. Dorothy Day saw war as an aberration that was opposed to active love. Her contribution to personalism was nonviolence. The *Catholic Worker* took a pacifist stance and maintained it.[16] In its beginning, the *Worker* had focused on work and unemployment; in the late 1930s and early 1940s, it was concerned about the buildup of armaments and the threat of war. Day condemned the "tribal morality" that had justified the dropping of the atom bomb and criticized the *New York Times* for espousing this morality. She tried to raise people's consciousness about nuclear madness.[17] In the late 1950s, she and others at the Catholic Worker refused to comply with the air-raid drills in New York City. They were arrested often and jailed several times (*Day*, 438–40).

In 1962, Dorothy helped begin the American Catholic organization of conscientious objectors known as the Pax Group, renamed Pax Christi in 1972, which opposed conscription. In the early 1960s, Catholic Worker peace activists burned their draft cards. In the fall of 1963, Dorothy spoke at Spode House in England at a British Catholic peace conference. In November 1965, she and A. J. Muste were principal speakers at an anti–Vietnam war demonstration. The main organization of the radical Catholic peace movement at this time was the Catholic Peace Fellowship, which reprinted articles by Day and other pacifists. On August 6, 1976, at the Catholic Eucharistic Congress, she reminded her audience that it was the day on which the United States had dropped the atom bomb on Hiroshima.[18]

Dorothy was considered a venerable leader of American pacifism, and of Catholic pacifism in particular. She voiced her opposition to armed resistance, violent revolution, and capital punishment. She was opposed to war because it sacrifices human freedom. She was aware that it is not enough to show people the suffering involved in war; religious conversion is necessary, that is to say, a falling in love with God that frees us to reach out to those who are in pain. She rejoiced that Vatican II passed the schema "The Church in the Modern World" with its unequivocal condemnation of nuclear warfare. She called peace the most important issue of our time (*Sixties*, 100, 236–37, 253, 278).

Commitment to the Struggle of Being a Woman of Faith: Builder of Community and of a Better World

Dorothy Day wrote as a woman of faith, with all the cares and responsibilities of a single parent as well as co-founder of the Catholic Worker movement. She wrote in a concrete and holistic way, steeped in the everyday events of her life. Her tone was conversational and her style was narrative. She could not be abstract nor speculative: "It is a woman's mind, and if my daily written meditations are of the people about me, of what is going on, — then it must be so. It is a part of every meditation to apply the virtue, the mystery, to the daily life we lead."[19]

She could not take time for prolonged prayer when her child was little; instead, she prayed when she awoke and off and on during the day: "Not in the privacy of a study — but here, there and everywhere — at the kitchen table, on the train, on the ferry, on my way to and from appointments and even while making supper or putting Teresa to bed" (*House*, 3). Given to self-criticism, she chided herself for her lack of recollection, her imperfections, her slow progress: "I do know how small I am and how little I can do and I beg You, Lord, to help me for I cannot help myself."[20]

Dorothy reflected on a mother's daily, selfless love for her children as a form of detachment from creatures and care for others. She compared women's bodies pregnant or dragged down by children to a cross to be carried. In fact, she called the suffering of childbirth woman's glory and the path of pain woman's lot. She asserted that a woman can live a deep spirituality and union with God through being a housewife and mother, although her work leaves her no time for self-development through prayer and reading. Day described a mother's mortification of the senses: eyes, nose, and ears exposed constantly to disorder and confusion, failing appetite, fatigue, weakness, and a solitude that cuts her off from conversation and music. A mother knows the beauty and joy of babies and small children, as well as the suffering, such as illnesses, night watches, contrariness, and infant perversities (*Pilgrimage*, 9–10).

At one point, Day recalled pictures she had of six generations of mothers and daughters in her own family, revealing her pride in being the woman she was. She reminisced poignantly about her mother's dying and death. When she wrote in the 1940s, she described woman as food provider and homemaker (*Pilgrimage*, 30–40, 163–65, 174). She affirmed a woman's ability to integrate the practical and the mystical when she wrote: "Meditations for woman, these notes should be called, jumping as I do from the profane to the sacred over and over. But then, living in the country, with little children, with growing things, one has the sacramental view of life" (*Pilgrimage*, 41).

From time to time, she felt discouraged and ineffective; she was full of self-doubt when she had to leave her daughter in others' hands. Instead of blaming others, she advocated mutual charity and self-criticism, trying to see the other's positive aspects (*House*, 170–72, 251–53). She was very conscious of her own faults and weaknesses, and sometimes held herself responsible for the deviant behavior of others, regretting that she had not loved them enough (*Pilgrimage*, 126; *Loaves*, 151–55, 176–78).

In writing the biography of Thérèse of Lisieux, she wrote as one woman of faith telling the story of another such woman. She did not write always in the third person, but sustained a genre of narrative where she would interject her own observations as a woman. She could not help noticing, for example, that the mother's position in that household was one of hard work while that of the man was more leisurely with time for travel, business contacts, and the life of the spirit (*Therese*, 55).

For the title of her autobiography, *The Long Loneliness*, she borrowed a phrase from another woman of faith, Mary Ward, English foundress of the Sisters of Loretto. Day felt that women especially are victims of the long loneliness and need a community. She experienced the human need for companionship as well as for God (*Loneliness*, 157–58). She knew that by laying down her life with others for others, she was making peace with herself, with her deepest womanly desires and needs.

She was opposed to the view of woman as plaything in favor of the view of woman as a person. By the 1960s, she supported working women who needed or wanted to work outside the home. She stayed with her grandchildren so that her daughter could train in practical nursing (*Sixties*, 159, 201–2). She provided a place where women can be themselves in their uniqueness, not identified by their relationships with men but rather by their radical commitment to the poor.[21]

In April 1963, she was one of seventy-five women belonging to ecumenical women's peace groups around the world who made a women's peace pilgrimage to Rome to thank John XXIII for his encyclical *Pacem in Terris*, (*Sixties*, 137–49). Then during Vatican II, in the fall of 1965, she made a second pilgrimage to Rome to participate in a ten-day fast for peace together with nineteen other women from all over the world, while members of peace groups lobbied for a strong antiwar statement in schema 13 of the "Pastoral Constitution on the Church in the Modern World" (*Sixties*, 240–52). These pilgrimages to Rome were efforts for making peace by networking among women of faith who knew themselves to be builders of a better world for all. In the fall of 1967, Dorothy made her third trip to Rome for the International Congress of the Laity to make her contribution as a laywoman in today's world (*Sixties*, 312, 317, 323).

She modeled a form of woman's power in the church today that was based on her personal experience. By claiming and trusting her own inner authority, she confronted issues of poverty, unemployment, and war with the courage of her convictions. She was self-directed and could stand up to authority, as when she wrote her editorials and took her stand for pacifism against the official church position. Her presence in the Catholic Worker movement enabled a community to be nurtured, a community that did not feed on itself but gave life to others by breaking bread with them. Her authority did not concentrate on asserting itself but rather on empowering others.[22] Her purpose in participating in strikes and demonstrations was always to show support for the workers in order that they could assume leadership among themselves in negotiating with employers.

Conclusion

Dorothy Day lived different lifestyles at different times of her life: the single life, a common-law marriage, single parent motherhood, and celibacy lived in community. She was a socialist in college and became a Catholic in 1927. She experienced arrest, strip search, imprisonment, abortion, and a suicide attempt. She knew the insecurities that poor people know: hunger, bitter cold, unemployment, changing employment, shame and self-contempt in jail, and unpaid bills. It became her call to find Christ in other people, especially in poor and destitute people. Not given to mystical visions, she kept alive her this-worldly vision of a better world, of improved conditions for workers, of bread for the hungry and homes for the homeless. She was not merely a writer dreaming dreams, but became a social worker for people she had never expected to welcome into her home. On the one hand, Dorothy was a radical, espousing unpopular views like pacifism and the right of workers to organize. On the other hand, she loved devotional practices like going to Benediction and praying the rosary. She modeled for Christian laypeople a life of prayer and service in the world.

She is a forerunner of liberation theology, political theology, and narrative theology. She knew the need Christians have to discover and reveal how God is acting in their lives, especially when they are poor and oppressed. But she also knew their need for people to mediate God's care and presence to them through the sharing of food, clothing, and shelter. Her call was to speak the word of God's love in deeds of love. Her solidarity with poor people was not a condescending method of handouts; she lived with them as they lived, eating the food cooked for them with them and wearing the clothes donated to them. Her own concerns were socio-political: unemployment, poverty, racism, and war. Like Teresa of Avila, she found God by reading the book of her life. She realized she could help make God accessible to others by writing in faith about her life.

At ease with herself, she felt comfortable serving lunch to the people of the street, making love to an atheist, and learning how to love in faith from a committed Christian. Having felt the wound of "the long loneliness," she felt an empathy with others that led her to respond by providing a community life for homeless people.

Dorothy Day is a peacemaker in our nuclear age. Committed to pacifism and nonviolence, she suffered the loss of volunteers and readers in order to be faithful to her vision. She networked with peace groups and, in particular, with groups of women committed to peace. She was consistent in her opposition to the draft, the atom bomb, and air-raid drills. She risked imprisonment several times when she demonstrated nonviolently against these features of our nuclear age, lest they become acceptable worldwide. She knew the power of the pen and used it as her "weapon" of peace to bring about peace.

Her spirituality is a mysticism of everyday life, of daily, selfless love for all people. She was a woman with a pierced heart, willing to be in touch with the pain and joy of her own heart and able to lead others to the core of their being. She experienced loneliness, disappointment, and the ingratitude of others as experiences of grace. She believed in the unity of love of neighbor and love of God. Dorothy Day opened herself to the mystery of God in her life and discovered that this mystery is

a forgiving nearness. In the strength of this discovery, she embraced
the message of Christ's redemptive love as she reached out to love the
unlovable. She mediated God's forgiving nearness by giving herself to
the workers and unemployed people who came for food and support.[23]
In the course of her growth in faith, she experienced grace as acceptance,
conversion, discipleship in community, and witness and service.[24]

In her life, her faith, and her writings, Dorothy Day embodied the
spirituality of the church of the future, a spirituality of the Sermon
on the Mount, a spirituality of hope, a spirituality of adoration not
degenerating to a horizontal humanism: hers was a spirituality that focused on the essentials found in the Christian tradition; it was based
on her solitary decision in faith; it fostered a community of shared
faith and goods in the Catholic Worker houses of hospitality; and it
had an ecclesial aspect of loving devotion to the church of sinners. Her
ecclesial sense led her to envision the shape of the church to come:
a church that is open, ecumenical, from the roots, democratized, and
socio-critical. That is to say, she was against a church with a ghetto
mentality that is closed to new ideas; she was in favor of people's cooperation in serving the world; she created basic communities of people
living, working, and praying together; she encouraged the participation
of the laity; her love of neighbor had a definite socio-political character since she believed in changing social institutions by starting new
ones.[25]

After a religious quest that lasted into her adult life, she became a
Roman Catholic and thereby joined a community of praise. She realized
in this way that she could satisfy her need to worship with other people
of the same faith. After a quest for her own identity, she allowed her
longing for love and companionship to be transformed into a commitment to community life, a community based on loving and serving the
hungry and homeless. In her passion for justice, she supported workers
in sit-down strikes and educated them to protect their rights and take
care of their needs. Her call to peacemaking included voluntary poverty. Through her editorial columns, her lectures, and her nonviolent
participation in demonstrations, she made efforts to bring about the
possibility of peace in our war-torn world. As a woman, she became not
only a mother, but also a believer and a builder of a better world for
all people.

She can be a spiritual guide for today. Her ability to balance her
life of prayer and praise with her commitment to social justice can
be a support to those who choose to serve the poor and oppressed.

Her willingness not only to feed and clothe the poor but also to live and eat with them validates the authenticity of her written word. Her acceptance of the paschal mystery of community life can strengthen those who choose to let their capacity for *eros* be transformed into *agape*. Her experience of how community heals the long loneliness can strengthen us to build a community of shared faith and shared goods in an era marked by individualism. She challenges North American consumerism by her radical poverty. Her clear vision of the cost of discipleship can shed light on our efforts to bring the gospel to bear on the reality of our daily life. She inspires us to see Christ in others. Her compassionate love of neighbor is her passionate love of God. Her conviction that global peace depends on making peace with ourselves and our neighbors provides the acid test for the peace movement. Her commitment to the struggle of being a woman of faith paved the way for her to exercise spiritual leadership among the men of the Bowery, her colleagues in the Catholic Worker movement, and many people throughout the world who saw her as a peacemaker in a nuclear age.

READINGS

Dorothy Day's autobiography is *The Long Loneliness* (San Francisco: Harper & Row, 1981). The story of the Catholic Worker movement is in *Loaves and Fishes* (San Francisco: Harper & Row, 1983). She wrote a book on Thérèse of Lisieux entitled *Therese* (Notre Dame: Fides, 1960).

A subscription to the *Catholic Worker* is available at: The Catholic Worker, 36 East First Street, New York, NY 10003. Many of her unpublished addresses can be obtained in written form or audio cassette by writing the Marquette University Archives, Marquette University, 1415 West Wisconsin Avenue, Milwaukee, WI 53233.

For background material on Dorothy Day, consult William D. Miller, *A Harsh and Dreadful Love: Dorothy Day and the Catholic Worker Movement* (New York: Liveright, 1973); *Dorothy Day: A Biography* (San Francisco: Harper & Row, 1982); and *All Is Grace: The Spirituality of Dorothy Day* (Garden City, N.Y.: Doubleday, 1987). For a detailed account of the development of the Catholic Worker movement, read Mel Piehl, *Breaking Bread: The Catholic Worker and the Origin of Catholic Radicalism in America* (Philadelphia: Temple University Press, 1982). Robert Coles, *A Spectacle unto the World: The Catholic Worker Move-*

ment (New York: Viking Press, 1973), provides a readable overview of the Catholic Worker movement. Robert Coles, *Dorothy Day: A Radical Devotion* (Reading, Mass.: Addison-Wesley, Merloyd Lawrence, 1987), gives a personable approach to her views and values, including passages from conversations that Coles had with Dorothy Day in 1970.

3
KARL RAHNER

(1904–1984)

Theologian of Everyday Christian Life

KARL RAHNER, a contemporary German Jesuit theologian, wrote theology for Christians living in the changing world today. Many of his theological insights have pastoral implications for our everyday lives.

He was born, one of seven children, in Freiburg im Breisgau, a city at the edge of the Black Forest and at that time part of the Grand Duchy of Baden. Hugo, his older brother, also entered the Society of Jesus and became a patristic theologian. Karl entered the Jesuits in 1922 and was ordained in 1932. He attended Martin Heidegger's courses and was influenced by the thought of Joseph Maréchal, S.J. Rahner taught theology in Innsbruck, Muenster, and Munich. He was a *peritus*, a theological consultant, at Vatican II. He wrote countless articles and books, including a twenty-two volume series called *Theological Investigations*. He died in Innsbruck in March 1984.

In this chapter, I discuss the following five attitudes of heart that Karl Rahner attributed to the practice of the Christian life: faith in God, living a mysticism of everyday life, prayer as surrender of the heart, love of neighbor as love of God, and hope for the future.

Faith in God: Trusting the Mystery

Rahner was convinced that faith in God means trusting the mystery. Faith cannot understand the incomprehensibility of God, but can find meaning in surrender.[1]

Rahner believed that to speak of the human is to speak of the divine and vice versa. He described God as the mystery in human experience. For him, then, God is the depth dimension in such experiences as solitude, friendship, community, death, and hope. This mystery discloses itself as a forgiving nearness, a hidden closeness, our real home, a love that shares itself, something familiar that we can turn to when we experience alienation in our own empty and perilous lives. Whenever we are in touch with ourselves authentically, we experience God.[2]

Over and over again, he insisted on the fundamental importance of the "givenness" of an authentic experience of God. He advised adoration of God for God's sake (*Dialogue*, 174-81, 328-30, 350-51; *Wintry*, 108). He insisted that it is not enough for us to learn about God from outside ourselves, the way we know about a country: "Whoever wants to live a convinced and genuine Christian life in the secularized desert where the God question is taboo must, therefore, want to be involved with God in the deepest experience of his or her person" (*Wintry*, 115).

Rahner raised the question of whether God can be addressed as a You. He recalled that God is not one object among many but rather the ultimate ground. He asserted that experiencing meaning and finality in freedom is an experience of God. Liturgy does not give us grace to go back into a godless world because the world is filled with God. His vision was of a world of grace.[3]

Rahner urged us to develop a faith that is open to unbelievers and open to challenge, a faith willing to be at risk. This faith is not merely the product of conceptual and institutional Christianity. It is a radically simple, transcendental faith that trusts in the mystery of God's power and mercy more than in the power of the church (*Belief*, 47-89).

We can abandon ourselves to mystery only where knowledge is taken up in love, because it is only in love that we can give ourselves over to the unknown. Mary, mother of God, is an example of this loving self-abandonment in faith.[4]

Rahner described our sole possession as solitariness before God, security in God's immediate presence. He was convinced that there will always be a mysticism of God's nearness. Finding God in all things lies at the heart of the Ignatian spirituality that Rahner considered a formative influence in his life and faith.[5]

He was especially concerned about Christianity's dialogue with atheism. He rejoiced that Vatican II granted that one can be an atheist without moral guilt and emphasized potential salvation for atheists.[6]

Respectful of the intellectual content of faith, he urged an intellectual integrity that believes with a responsible conscience. With Karl-Heinz Weger, S.J., Rahner wrote *Our Christian Faith: Answers for the Future*. They wrote for intelligent, skeptical Christians overcome with meaninglessness about a credible God, whom they saw as an invisible gardener who does not intervene in world processes and whose action is imperceptible (*Christian Faith*, 51-69).

This attitude of faith in God as mystery has practical implications for Christian living. First, it suggests to us that we get in touch with human events and experiences because speaking of the human is a way of speaking of the divine. To describe a moment of deep joy or deep pain is already to be talking about God. Second, it allows us to trust our experience of God as the touchstone for interpreting our lives and beliefs. We deepen our belief in God by articulating and celebrating God's presence in simple ways.

Living a Mysticism of Everyday Life: Experiences of Grace

For Rahner, every Christian is called to a mysticism of everyday faith, hope, and love, that differs not in kind but in degree from the extraordinary experiences of recognized mystics. We can discover and respond to God in ordinary situations like drinking a cup of tea or taking a walk. Our everyday faith is a faith that loves the earth. This is the source of Rahner's prediction that "the devout Christian of the future will either be a 'mystic' . . . or will cease to be anything at all."[7]

Mystical experience includes a going out of the self and a return to the self that may at times be expressed in visions, ecstasies, raptures, and locutions. But it is important to distinguish between the divine initiative and human subjectivity in these extraordinary phenomena. A person's core religious experience is more fundamental than phenomena that may accompany it. That is to say, the description and interpretation of these phenomena may reflect "historical inaccuracy, theological distortions and errors, partiality, or bad taste" (*Visions*, 64).[8]

Rahner wrote often about experiencing graced moments of God's seeming absence. This implies experiencing God in moments of silent forgiveness, solitude, joy, and loyalty, as well as letting go of false images of God. He affirmed the presence of the Spirit when we feel hope in disappointment, when we continue to carry responsibility even though we no longer feel successful or useful, when we freely accept the choice of our death, when we endure trying events patiently, when we continue to pray silently in darkness, and when we feel consoled by hoping. He enumerated other experiences of the Spirit when he wrote of our being patient, omitting an excuse, being faithful when prayer is dry, loving people who get on our nerves, refraining from complaint and self-praise, appreciating an ordinary song, seeing, and hearing. We all can discover that seeing, laughter, eating, and sleep are experiences of grace. We can also find that grace is at work when we choose silence instead of self-defense, forgiveness instead of resentment, a thankless sacrifice instead of inner satisfaction, a lonely decision of integrity instead of self-justification, perseverance in the love of God instead of control. The silent coming of God happens, for example, when a sick person surrenders to God in solitude, when a person tries to serve others through research, and when a person is drawn to repentance. Loneliness, disappointment, and the ingratitude of others can be graced moments because they open us to the transcendent. The silence of God, the toughness of life, and the darkness of death can all be graced events.[9]

In *Belief Today*, Rahner explored a theology of everyday things that does not try to make every day a holy day, that values the commonness of everyday things as a revelation of God's mystery, and that honors everyday things on Sundays. Admitting the monotony of our work, we can choose to work in Christ, letting God form in us patience, faithfulness, and unselfishness. Realizing that rest can be another form of activity, we can cultivate a habit of peaceful reflection through the appreciation of art, music, and insight for their own sake. He predicted that this "mysticism" of everyday life would be seen to be the essence of Christianity (*Belief*, 13–43, 78–79).

For Rahner, mysticism is the hidden experience of transcendence in everyday life, the experience of the Holy Spirit, the discovery of God in all things. It is a radical experience of faith that transcends concepts and categories. He claimed that Christians need to become mystics, to enter into a direct relationship with God, to concentrate on the basic elements of Christian living. He was concerned about the plight of ordinary Christians who experience neither their own subjectivity nor God's self-communication in daily affairs.[10]

A mysticism of daily living means finding God in all things. It means living as we want to be at our death, peaceful and surrendered. This is a wintry piety that can say in life as in death, hoping against hope: "Into your hands I commend my spirit" (*Dialogue*, 297).

Rahner's broad approach to mysticism sheds light on certain aspects of a mysticism of everyday life. First, it helps us to describe religious experiences not in terms of how unusual or colorful they may be, but rather in terms of how they inspire and strengthen us to live with greater faith, hope, and love. His approach also urges us to distinguish between people's core religious experience and the phenomena that may accompany an experience. For example, people may describe or edit their description of an experience of God in which they claim to have been given a locution or a vision. It is more difficult to assess the authenticity of a particular locution or vision than to affirm the authenticity of a person's basic holiness and religious experience. This approach may help people to focus on the fruits of their encounter with God, not the phenomena that may accompany it.

Third, Rahner's clarification invites us to affirm, express, and celebrate our experiences of the mystery of God in our daily lives. Mysticism is not limited to those technically called mystics in Christian tradition. It is possible for everyone. We live in a world of grace. We are invited to discover God's presence in the simple deeds of life.

Fourth, such an approach expands the notion of religious experience beyond the practice of formal prayer and the asceticism of daily life. If God is not only the mystery we meet in our prayer but also the mystery we experience in our life, then we need to live and reflect on the details of our daily lives in faith in order to know how God is acting. God can also be experienced in a novel, a play, a homily, a conversation with a friend, an issue, or on a vacation.

Fifth, it implies that we cannot limit God's presence to experiences that are tangibly filled with consolation. We also need to recognize the experience of the Spirit in life's search and struggle.

Prayer as Surrender of the Heart: Encounters with Silence

Rahner pointed us to the mystery of the heart, which, for him, is the symbol of the center of the person. It is the place where our freedom, consciousness, and affectivity most intimately dwell in an embodied way.[11]

As the center of freedom, the heart is the place of our surrender to the mystery of God. In the same manner, the heart of Christ is the center of his freedom, the place of his surrender to the mystery of God. As we surrender ourselves in adoration of God and compassion for others, we become women and men of the pierced heart.[12]

The heart is the place of our encounter with God, our "encounters with silence." It is the place where we experience our need for God.

Prayer is the opening of the heart to God. Loving prayer is the surrender of the heart to the incomprehensible mystery of God. Our relationship with God is nourished by our formal prayer and by our daily lives: we are to pray in everyday life, and we are to make everyday life our prayer.[13]

In his book *On Prayer*, Rahner called prayer one of the essentials of our life. When we are given peace in the awareness of our nothingness, we are drawn beyond the formulae of prayer to silent communion in the sense of God's presence and our dependence: "This colloquy of the heart with God cannot be expressed in words, because it is a silent reaching out toward God with reverential fear and sublime trust. It is a complete silent oblation of self, and an entire surrender to God" (*Prayer*, 15). He pointed to Christ in his agony, whose sense of abandonment by God can guide us to pray in dryness, weariness, and darkness: "The Garden of Olives was the desolation of Christ in order that it might become the consolation of all human desolation, for Christ is the living heart of the world."[14] Our self-realization depends on our acceptance of God's presence in our lives. The Holy Spirit is light in our darkness, source of our prayer, and our help in prayer. If we keep our minds and hearts on God, we will be sustained by the power of grace even in the midst of misery and disappointment. Rahner described three types of the prayer of decision: prayer in temptation which begs for strength and enlightenment, prayer in crisis asking for the courage to take responsibility for our world, and prayer in the hour of death commending ourselves into the hands of God.[15]

Rahner asked whether people praying today talk to themselves. He granted the personal involvement of God, but wondered about God's obscurity and silence. To the question of whether God actually says something to us in prayer, he answered that God speaks the word of our real self to us; we do not hear something in addition to ourselves, but we hear ourselves through God's word. In this context, our prayer of concrete petitions may be our way of mediation between the openness in which we experience ourselves and God. This prayer of petition can be viewed as symbolic of our surrender to God's will.[16]

Prayer, according to Rahner, strengthens us to bear one another's burdens and live together as true members of the body of Christ. He refused to support a spirituality that becomes too sophisticated for such devotional practices as rosaries, crucifixes, visits to the Blessed Sacrament, and night prayers. He urged the unity between prayer and life, prayer and work, prayer alone and prayer together, prayer of adoration and prayer of intercession. He encouraged us to ask the angels and saints

to intercede for us, keeping very clear that there is only one mediator,
Jesus Christ, but many mediations.[17]

Rahner called prayer the fundamental act of human existence. He
reminded us that prayer cannot be analyzed like an object of functional,
working knowledge. Nor is it reserved thereby to the realm of dreams
and emotions. He made a distinction between the analytical knowledge
of the scientist and the intuitive knowledge of the poet and the mystic.
Prayer for him is a contemplative knowledge of ourselves, God, others,
and the world.[18]

Prayer opens our heart to the mystery of the human condition. By
prayer, Rahner does not mean "the private luxury of cultivating a beautiful soul. It must be wrung from the cruelty of life by the deeds and the
anguish of faith" (*Servants*, 68). He proposed two ways to develop openness of heart. One is to surrender to God without fear of the loneliness
and powerlessness within. The other is to notice God's presence in one's
despair, in the silence of one's heart. It is to God our heart speaks. In response to the question of why God allows us to suffer, Rahner reviewed
the pious answers usually given and then admitted he did not know the
answer: he only knew that our surrender to the incomprehensible mystery of suffering is a form of surrender to the incomprehensible mystery
of God.[19]

Rahner believed that petitionary prayer actualizes the incomprehensibility of human existence that comes from and goes to God. Prayer as
surrender to God's will is meaningful as the bridge reconciling the incomprehensibility of human existence with its ultimate meaningfulness
(*Christian Faith*, 64, 67). He called the "acceptance of the unaccept-
able" redemptive since in it we are revealed as accepted and loved by
God (*Sacraments*, 30).

Rahner cautioned his readers against considering the length of routine prayer a measure of zeal or neglect in the spiritual life. Prayer can
be a means to radical self-surrender to God. He urged spiritual directors
to learn more about psychology in order to know the preconditions for
meditation, and he chided them for not reflecting on their own experience in prayer and communicating it to others. Just as action can be
prayer, so prayer can be action in the sense of trust in God, patience,
and love. He urged the sick person to live with the words of Jesus in
his dying: questioning God who had seemingly forsaken him and commending his spirit to God (*Opportunities*, 58-60, 75, 135-38). He called
prayer the "self-awareness of selfless love," which identifies with Jesus
in his surrender to God at death for love of others.[20]

Prayer invites us to surrender our hearts to God. One of Rahner's most powerful insights is that the more dependent we become on God, the more autonomous we become. That is to say, the more we turn to God who is the source of our freedom and identity, the more we become who we really are. Rahner called the heart the center of freedom and of surrender, since it is the place where we turn to God and choose in faith to give ourselves to God. All real prayer was for him the prayer of the heart in the sense that the heart is the place of our yearning for God, the place of our dependence on God, the place of our need for God.[21] This surrender to God in view of the incomprehensible mystery of human existence was for him a basic characteristic of Christianity (*Wintry*, 108-9).

Rahner's view of prayer can influence the way we engage in Christian commitment. First, it suggests that the heart is the center of freedom and not only the center of affectivity, and that we need to make choices of the heart based on gospel values. Through the support and challenge of a community of shared faith, we can become interiorly free to respond in the light of our call to be ourselves and to follow Jesus rather than simply to react to people and situations.

Second, it invites us to view God's will not as a prestructured plan in the mind of God, but rather as God's deep desire that we become our real selves. This means that our way of getting in touch with what God wants is getting in touch with what we most deeply want. A consequence of this attitude is that we consider providence a dialogue between two freedoms, human and divine. Rahner realized that we need to avoid a too facile interpretation of God's will, and at the same time to pray over events that are revelatory of God's presence and guidance. Third, this view suggests that since the heart is the place of our surrender to God, then it is important to be in touch with its movements. The Ignatian tradition of spiritual guidance emphasizes the place of discernment of spirits in enabling one to become contemplative in action. Spiritual direction, then, cannot consist only of a summary of lights received during formal prayer or a review of scriptural texts over which one has prayed. It involves discussing the attractions and resistances that constitute the dynamics of a person's relationship with God.

Fourth, this view of prayer shapes our dialogue with God. This dialogue is not chatter with God, the ritual of saying rote prayers to God, the routine of reading Scriptures at God. Rather, it is our attention to the revelation of who we really are and of who God really is in encounters with silence.

Fifth, it helps us to see that prayer can help us know and accept ourselves, God, others, and the world. The integrity and authenticity of our prayer reflect our self-knowledge and self-acceptance. It is in prayer that we can let go of our need to understand and to analyze. And it is in prayer that we can surrender to the mystery of the human condition, trusting that God is acting.

Sixth, if the more dependent we become on God the more autonomous we become, then prayer and spiritual direction can help free us as persons. This trust in God springs from a healthy self-confidence that relies on inner resources rather than the approval of others.

Love of Neighbor as Love of God: Love of Jesus

Rahner was convinced of the priority of God's love for us (*TI 6*, 231–49; *Opportunities*, 62–73). His conviction is that God is not one object of our love next to other objects of our love, but rather the horizon of our love. God is not a concrete You among others.

Our daily, humble love of others is our way of growing closer to God. Rahner insisted that the love of neighbor and the love of God mutually condition each other. The emptying of self is not "accomplished by practising pure inwardness, but by the real activity which is called humility, service, love of our neighbor, the cross and death" (*Visions*, 14). The experience of love is for Rahner an experience of God. By love, he means not only responding to others' needs but also being valued and valuing the other. In God's gift of self to us and in our gift of self to others, we experience our unconditional worth.[22]

Rahner recognized the need for a more profound theology of the love of neighbor as the existential experience of our relationship to Christ: "What is done to our neighbor really happens to Christ and is not merely interpreted as happening to Christ" (*Opportunities*, 61). He returned again and again to the notion that we love God and Jesus by loving our neighbor.[23] Christian love is redemptive through the acts of individuals loving without reward or reassurance, being faithful to the truth and to conscience, and accepting death in self-surrendering trust (*Commitment*, 75–113).

Meditating with those in prison chaplaincy on the text of Matthew 25:34–46, he questioned what it means to find Christ in prisoners.

He concluded that it means a reverent humility in face of another human being and a raw faith in God's presence when all we feel is the disappointment and loneliness of loving without return, reward, or gratitude. We not only find Christ but also find ourselves when we see in prisoners the truth of who we are: sinful and redeemed, enslaved and freed, not so different from those we visit (*Marketplace*, 61–79).

Rahner approached Jesus as the neighbor *par excellence*, affirming the centrality and significance of a personal relationship with Jesus. We are dealing with Jesus when we throw our arms around him. When we love Jesus, we love an actual human being: "We seek him, think about him, speak with him, we feel his nearness."[24] In loving Jesus, we identify with his destiny and commitment to God. We seek to meet Jesus in our neighbor and in the whole of our lives (*Prayers*, 77–82). There is a mystical and a societal component in following Jesus: a personal experience of God and the motivation to work for social justice. The notion of love of neighbor includes our global neighbors.[25] I call Rahner's description of the love of neighbor a contemporary form of devotion to the Sacred Heart. He perceived that the unity of the love of neighbor and the love of God is the essence of a theology of devotion to the Sacred Heart.[26]

A conviction about the unity of the love of neighbor and the love of God can affect our relationships with others. If God is the horizon of our love, then the love of neighbor is not in conflict or in competition with the love of God: they are one love. We need not set up a false dichotomy between formal prayer and service. If we are striving to do God's will, we only need to ask ourselves: what is the loving response to make in this situation? This question becomes more complex in view of the many social concerns that demand our decisions, based on both faith and justice. Second, if love has to do with self-emptying, then we need to ask ourselves just how loving is our heart, especially in responding to people whom we find hard to love. As we empty ourselves of expectations, disappointments, and prejudices, we become open to receive the other as other. Third, in order to love others, we need to love ourselves, to value ourselves, and to find our self-esteem in our relationship with God and with others. Fourth, prayer and spiritual direction together can foster our personal love for Jesus by inviting us to share more and more of ourselves with him, needing him totally and trusting him radically.

Hope for the Future:
Taking Responsibility for Church and World

Rahner urged us to love the church, to view the church not only as the church of saints, but also as the church of sinners who know their need for God. He urged a conversion from a narrow, introspective, individualistic kind of Christianity to a broad, ecumenical, communitarian kind that is open to the Spirit at all levels of church life and practice. In faith and hope, with a loyal affection for the church and a critical realism about its structures, he sketched his vision of the shape of the church to come. He saw that the situation of the global humanity of today calls for a world church and new opportunities for intercommunication leading to genuine Christian communion. He realized that the call to participate in the church's mission to the world implies the call to take political responsibility. He supported the efforts of basic Christian communities to build communion.[27]

Karl Rahner made a significant contribution as theological advisor at Vatican II. Just before the council, he had been partially silenced by Rome, that is, forbidden to write except under Roman censorship. He suffered personally from the church for which he took such courageous responsibility.[28]

The Second Vatican Council was just the beginning of a growing awareness of the church as a global reality with pluralistic theologies and diverse forms of worship. Rahner was convinced that the church in the contemporary world must live its mission of mediating the Spirit of worship and hope in the midst of secularism and humanism. For him, Christianity today has two components, mystical and societal. External indoctrination cannot substitute for the immediate experience of God's nearness, and the love of neighbor is not credible unless it includes compassion for and critique of society with attending political implications (*Dialogue*, 46–53, 181–85).

He called the world the event of the self-communication of God, and the church a community excluding no one and proclaiming an absolute hope, the sacrament of salvation for all the world. He recognized that faith today cannot be private inwardness but must assume active responsibility for the world (*Servants*, 16–17, 23, 43, 68).

After Vatican II, Rahner exhorted Christians to take their responsibility for their church in a time of transition. Faithful to tradition and open to risk, the church is a church of sinners living in a diaspora in which clergy and laity are called to love God while fulfilling the family, professional, and civic duties of their secular life. He described a positive relationship between faith and a secular culture. When treating the delicate balance between commitment to the church and personal freedom, he gave as an example the necessity of private and liturgical prayer. He explored the meaning of true freedom, not as a choice between objects but as the fundamental option of choosing or rejecting God.[29]

Rahner also spoke of the danger of reducing religion to political activity and the relationship with God to fellow-feeling. But he was increasingly conscious of the socio-political implications of living as a Christian in today's world. He spoke of peace as a mandate, as the work of justice. Working for peace is learning to see the institutionalized injustices of our society, overcoming the temptation to take refuge in privacy, improving the political climate, and breaking down the fronts between political parties. He gave some examples of taking responsibility for the world: overcoming group selfishness, choosing not to take from Third World countries more than they receive from us, and respecting the right to conscientious objection. The lover of peace is one who is willing to change a view, to accept defeat in a division of opinion, to admit an opponent to be in the right, to be polite and patient with someone who is irritating. He urged creative work for peace in the form of concrete action rather than abstract anticipation. He suggested ways for church leaders to take co-responsibility for the church: their duty to discuss with one another subjects like the possibility of married clergy and their willingness to risk creative and responsible experimentation in the church.[30]

Emphasizing the individual Christian's responsibility for the life of the church, Rahner affirmed the layperson's right to free speech in the church and encouraged laity to make their views known and to take personal responsibility for pastoral action. He viewed the church as sacrament of salvation and predicted that the church of the future would be more personal and would acknowledge unbaptized people who seek God. Rahner hoped that the spirituality of the church of the future would concentrate on the essential elements of Christianity: God, Jesus, the church, grace, and human freedom.[31]

This hope is a challenge to create our own happiness and free ourselves by letting go of all securities as we learn to live in the darkness of God (*Practice*, 249). Rahner spelled out what he meant by this hope for the future in his dialogue with Pinchas Lapide: "I hope for the final self-communication of God face-to-face. For me, that is the absolute future."[32]

He considered nuclear war morally reprehensible and disarmament absolutely necessary, and urged Christian countries to take the first step toward disarmament in the spirit of the gospel. Rahner gave a 1984 lecture on realistic humanism at an international conference on peace and nuclear war. He recognized certain human convictions that Marxists and Christians hold in common: the obligation for common dialogue, the responsibility to prevent the world's destruction and promote world peace, and respect for human freedom. While urging us as Christians to be involved in a more radical way than other communities with the struggle for peace and justice, he also invited us to be calm and patient with the scandals and bourgeois mentality of the church since we are all sinners. Peacemaking includes patient acceptance of the humanity of the church. Disillusionment about church hierarchy, for example, need not mean leaving the church, but rather living within limits and acting assertively with hope in the future.[33]

How can our prayer life influence our response? For Rahner, our life of prayer makes us more open and more free, but not necessarily more enlightened about how to solve the problems of our world. Second, he warned that turning to God can seem to reduce religion to "the opium of the people," but in truth religion does not take away our helplessness nor our secular problems. In other words, surrender to God does not guarantee that everything will work out well. Here, Rahner is a strong spiritual guide urging us to a radical realism about our life with God in the world.[34]

Rahner's dreams for the future have implications for the practice of faith. Hope for a world-church means that inculturation must be implemented much more conscientiously in order that all may feel free to worship and live in faith according to their culture, perhaps non-European culture, not according to Romanized traditions. Hope for an ecumenical unity of the churches invites us to dialogue more seriously with our fellow Christians. A conviction about the universal possibility of salvation can allow Christians to respect the integrity of atheists and agnostics. Acceptance of such a church means a declericalization in attitudes as well as in structures. It also means active lay participation in church life. Living as a committed Christian in the world today is a twofold task: remaining receptive to experience the mystery at the heart of our life and taking active responsibility for the fate of the earth.

Conclusion

Rahner was not only a great Roman Catholic theologian, but also a spiritual guide for today. His spirituality and theology are based on the primacy of religious experience. He was convinced that we are given experiences of the Spirit in our lives through the paschal mystery of our hopes and disappointments. His enthusiastic realism about the following of Jesus included both a personal relationship with Jesus and a social, even socio-political, dimension. Over and over again, he urged simple fidelity to duty and daily, humble love.

Some of Rahner's theological insights are relevant for the practice of the Christian life in today's secular world. His contemplative approach to the mystery of God in human experiences can enable those of us who are convinced that we live in a world of grace to speak of God in secular terms. His understanding of the Christian life as a mysticism of everyday life can free us to seek and find God not only in times of formal prayer, but also in times of suffering, celebration, service, and self-emptying, all of which we can view as opportunities for faith. His experience of prayer as surrender of the heart can help us to concentrate on the fruits of prayer, the ways in which we let go of all that keeps us from being open to experience the mystery of God in our lives. His conviction about the unity of the love of neighbor and the love of God can validate our earnest search for faith and justice. This search stretches our love of neighbor beyond local and national boundaries to include global concerns, and strengthens our hope for the future of the church and of the world.

Rahner contemplated the mysteries of human existence, such as love and suffering, in the light of faith. Hence for Rahner, love is surrender to the mystery of God, and true love of God is inseparable from love of the neighbor. Suffering is not punishment for sin nor some hardship imposed on the strong who alone have the courage to bear it. Suffering remains a mystery to which one brings not a solution but surrender in the constantly renewed gift of one's heart to God in union with the passion and death of Christ.

His writings on the church before and after Vatican II helped Christians feel comfortable with belonging to a church in diaspora, becoming a church open to unbelievers, and building a community of shared faith and collaboration among laity, priests, and bishops. His phrase "Christian in the marketplace" helped many to deepen their life of faith in their place of work as well as in their place of rest and formal prayer. His conviction that the church is the sacrament of the world's salvation presented a humbler image more acceptable to non-Christians. Rahner was strongly committed to ecumenism and keenly aware of its opportunity for dialogue and collaboration.[35]

A pastoral theologian, Rahner was eager that Christianity be credible to the person of today. He undertook what James Bacik calls the key pastoral task today, that is, helping people to contemplate the mystical dimension of the Christian faith expressed in its central doctrines.[36] Rahner was so committed to the challenge of living the theology he taught that Johannes Metz has spoken of Rahner's life as a theological life and Rahner's theology as mystical biography.[37]

His preaching and writing reflected a fidelity to Scripture and tradition. He was loyal to the church, even as he argued against conceptual and institutional Christianity that loses touch with the message of Christianity by its structures and systems. A Christian of intellectual integrity, he found ways to make the good news intelligible to intelligent believers and to show the compatibility of faith and intellectual integrity (*Belief*, 93–128).

Karl Rahner is a spiritual guide for today. His sense of God invites us to balance a deep reverence for God's absolute mystery with a faith in God's forgiving nearness. His sense of Christ challenges us to set aside theological concepts and open ourselves to a personal relationship with Jesus that is not private or sentimental, but communal and redemptive. His sense of the church condemns our triumphalism and false security, broadening us to welcome a church of the laity, a church of sinners accepting all as weak human beings. His sense of grace penetrates our world of everyday things and discovers the Spirit at work even in solitude and loneliness, in work and rest, in disappointment and in the ingratitude of others. His sense of faith clothes us afresh in deeds of selfless love.

A man of prayer and a priest, Rahner invited fellow believers to let God speak to them the word they are, the truth of their being. He urged them to share their struggle to find God in a secularized world.

A Jesuit, Rahner focused on the dignity of human freedom in dialogue with God's freedom. He preached Ignatian retreats that emphasized human experience as a locus of God's presence, the human person as a mystery oriented by transcendence to the mystery of God, and God as the mystery at the heart of human existence.

A theologian, he led others not to the formulae of faith but to the mystery of God, not to the articulation of concepts but to the acceptance of grace. Overwhelmed by the transcendence of God, he was a theologian of grace, of God's forgiving nearness.

For him, the church is a world-church. Convinced that the Roman Catholic Church experienced itself for the first time as a world-church at Vatican II, he goaded the church to shoulder its responsibilities and global concerns by de-Romanizing creeds, liturgical cults, and moral codes in order to attain true inculturation. Convinced that the church would be a diaspora church, a remnant church, he helped Catholics to feel comfortable with their solitary decision in faith and to build communion with other Christians.

Rahner knew that faith in God meant living in mystery. The love of neighbor is the acid test of the love of God and the love of Jesus. Prayer means surrendering the heart to God. Steeped in the Ignatian spirituality of the contemplative in action, he could see that the attitudes of heart we need for surrender in prayer are the same as those needed for surrender in life situations: patience, trust, and sacrifice. Hope for the future implies responsibility for the church and the world. Challenged by political and liberation theology, he began to reflect on the socio-political implications of living Christianity in the contemporary world, suggesting structures that would favor dialogue between clergy and laity, between Christians and unbelievers.

Rahner broadened the notion of mysticism to include experiences of the Holy Spirit in our daily lives. For him, mysticism is not esoteric visions and ecstasies reserved to a few individual Christians, but rather an encounter with the depth-dimension at the heart of our existence.

He broadened the notion of grace to include not only tangible moments of God's intimacy, but also ambiguous moments of God's presence in seeming absence: loneliness, disappointment, and the ingratitude of others.

He broadened our notion of the unity of the love of neighbor and the love of God. Instead of mouthing pious words about finding Christ in the other, he perceived that it is precisely in the void created by loving another person without reward or satisfaction of any kind that we experience the infinite mystery of God.

Rahner challenged us to bridge the gap between the theology we read and the lives we live. His integrity evokes our own. His keen awareness of God's mysterious absence can shed light on God's mysterious presence in our lives. His conviction that to speak of the human is to speak of the divine can encourage us to encounter God in our secular world and to talk of God in secular language. His insistence on letting religious experience be the point of departure for theological reflection calls us to treasure and name daily experiences of grace.

Inspired by Rahner's vision, we take our responsibility as adult committed Christians in the church today. We are to witness to gospel values with each action, preach the word of God in every attitude of heart, and work always for the greater glory of God in the marketplace.

READINGS

For an overview of the main lines of Rahner's spirituality, see *The Practice of Faith: A Handbook of Contemporary Spirituality*, ed. Karl Lehmann and Albert Raffelt (New York: Crossroad, 1986), and *Prayers for a Lifetime*, ed. Albert Raffelt (New York: Crossroad, 1984). For a taste of his mysticism of everyday life, read *Belief Today: Theological Meditations*, ed. Hans Küng (New York: Sheed & Ward, 1967); *Everyday Faith*, trans. W. J. O'Hara (New York: Herder & Herder, 1968); and *Opportunities for Faith: Elements of a Modern Spirituality*, trans. Edward Quinn (New York: Seabury, Crossroad, 1974).

I Remember: An Autobiographical Interview with Meinold Krauss (New York: Crossroad, 1985) gives Rahner's version of his life. *Is Christian Life Possible Today?* (Denville, N.J.: Dimension Books, 1984) gives Rahner's responses to questions about living Christianity raised by young adults and teenagers.

For a valuable treatment of key themes in his spirituality, consult Norman J. King, *Encountering God All Ways and Every Day* (Minneapolis: Winston Press, 1982). For an excellent pastoral rendering of Rahner's notion of mystery, see James J. Bacik, *Apologetics and the Eclipse of Mystery: Mystagogy according to Karl Rahner* (Notre Dame: University of Notre Dame Press, 1980). In *Transforming Grace: Christian Tradition and Women's Experience* (San Francisco: Harper & Row, 1988), Anne E. Carr has put aspects of Karl Rahner's thought in dialogue with feminism.

Robert Kress, *A Rahner Handbook* (Atlanta, Ga.: John Knox Press, 1982), and Herbert Vorgrimler, *Understanding Karl Rahner: An Introduction to His Life and Thought* (New York: Crossroad, 1986), provide helpful background information.

4
SIMONE WEIL

(1909–1943)

Witness to Solidarity in Affliction

SIMONE WEIL is a witness to solidarity in affliction and a voice for afflicted people everywhere.

A French Jew born in 1909, she became a philosopher and author with a passion for truth and justice. She labored as a factory worker and fought in the Spanish civil war. In the spring of 1942, during the World War II Nazi occupation of France, she and her parents went to the United States. She returned to join the Free French in London, in a vain effort to work with the Resistance in France. She was treated for tuberculosis, but even in the sanitarium refused to eat more than her people in France could eat on war rations. She died in 1943 of tuberculosis and malnutrition at the age of thirty-four.

She is a spiritual guide for us today by reason of her passion for truth and justice and by her choice to become other-centered. She suffered from migraine headaches, loneliness, the temptation to suicide, and the consequences of denial of her body. Through her weakness and brokenness, she experienced the lot of the afflicted.[1]

Her life and thought are counter-cultural. They pose the following questions: How can solidarity with the afflicted be an alternative to a competitive relationship with others? In multinational corporations that reward executive positions, can we respect the dignity of the worker? In war-torn countries, can we still struggle for international peace? What can Weil's insistence on "paying attention" teach us about centering our multifaceted interests and concerns? What does waiting for God have to say to North Americans who are driven to seek quick solutions and taught by their culture to expect them — one-hour service, fast food, the fax machine?

This chapter is not a comprehensive survey of her thought, but rather presents five attitudes of heart that mark her life and writings:

solidarity with afflicted people, respect for the dignity of the worker, struggle for international peace, attention, and waiting.[2]

Solidarity in Affliction: Redemptive Suffering

Simone Weil's life and writings reflected her consistent solidarity with afflicted people: factory workers, peasant farmers, and victims of totalitarian governments. She called solidarity in affliction "redemptive suffering." But she did not consider affliction in itself redemptive suffering. Affliction, *malheur*, was for her more preoccupying and debilitating than suffering, since it includes social degradation. According to Weil, to experience empathy with afflicted people, we need to have been afflicted at one time. Only then can we be united in common support of their rights. This solidarity with afflicted people can involve the pain of struggling to improve their lot or trying to walk with them in their misery. Such suffering can be redemptive, that is, life-giving for others.

For Weil, affliction, *malheur*, is characterized by three elements that are co-constitutive: physical pain, psychological distress, and social degradation. It leads to a sense of God's absence, hardness of heart, discouragement, scorn for other afflicted people, and complicity in one's own affliction. It is impossible for the afflicted to feel compassion. In other words, if one is not afflicted, one cannot know what it is like to be afflicted; if one is afflicted, one cannot reach out to others in affliction since one's own state is so miserable. This situation reinforces the afflicted person's sense of isolation. Affliction is anonymous, depriving its victims of their personality. It is not chosen but endured.

The crucifixion is Christ's affliction for the love of God. It is wrong to desire affliction because it is often suffered unwillingly; if it comes, however, it can be experienced as a participation in Christ's passion, whereby we share in the distress of the abandoned Christ's distance from God. In fact, the only way we can be strengthened to accept real affliction and to love in affliction with the love of God is by contemplating Christ's Cross. Simone Weil's radical insight into the negative and positive value of affliction can contribute to our lived experience, and to the Christian understanding and celebration of the paschal mystery.[3]

She wrote of God's self-emptying, taking the form of a slave in Christ. For her, creation, the passion, and the Eucharist are all aspects of this movement of God's withdrawal and abandonment. Creation is, then, God's loving self-renunciation.[4]

When Weil began to teach philosophy at a lycée for girls in Le Puy in 1931, she supported the social, political, and economic claims of the struggling working class and was an active member of two teachers' unions: the reformist Confédération générale du Travail (CGT) and the communist-dominated Confédération générale du Travail unitaire (CGTU). She wrote for three publications and made a weekly trip to St. Etienne, fifty miles away, to work with a revolutionary syndicalist group and with the trade union organization of that region.[5]

After teaching philosophy for three years, Simone chose to live the life and do the work of an unskilled factory worker. Her "Factory Journal" bears startling testimony to her commitment to this gesture of solidarity, in spite of physical and psychological difficulties on the job. During this year, she developed experientially her notion of what it means to be a slave, unable to rebel yet unwilling to submit. She considered herself "a beast of burden" and "the victim designated for any harsh blow" (*Writings*, 155–226). In letters, she wrote of factory work as a contact with real life, admitting at the same time that in actuality it was exhausting and humiliating; it involved a slavery based on passive obedience and the necessity for speed, which tended to prevent revolt (*Letters*, 10–12, 19–22, 35).

Reduced to the condition of a slave with no respect or rights, she concluded that workers would never be capable of revolution as long as their oppression was reinforced by humiliation and subservience. Between December 1934 and August 1935, she held three different jobs as an unskilled factory worker. In this experience, Weil identified experientially with the suffering she strove to overcome. She saw the affliction about which she later wrote. She reached the point where the work caused her such preoccupation and strain that she could no longer think (*Writings*, 171).

Weil realized the impotence of factory workers in these conditions, allowed not to complain but to be compliant (*Writings*, 203, 213). Reflecting on her experience, she wrote that she had felt that she did not possess any rights. What struck her most forcibly was the destruction of any feeling of self-respect. She concluded: "The main fact isn't the suffering but the humiliation."[6]

Weil continued her solidarity with afflicted people even when she stopped being a worker. She wrote letters to a factory manager with suggestions for improvement and corresponded with a manager of electrical companies to seek employment and report on workers' conditions (*Letters*, 23–69).

In the fall of 1940, as a Jew forbidden to teach, she found herself in the south of France where she met and got to know Joseph-Marie Perrin, O.P., with whom she discussed her attraction and resistance to Catholicism, and Gustave Thibon who got her a job as a farm laborer and arranged for her lodging and work. In the spring of 1942, she and her parents went to the United States; from there she joined the Free French in London in a vain effort to work with the Resistance in France.

In 1942, she wrote to Joë Bousquet, a man paralyzed in World War I, that war is affliction.[7] Physical pain makes us think of affliction and opens us to the seed of divine love that can grow and bear fruit in patience. She tried to comfort him by observing that those who experience the same kind of affliction that the world feels have the opportunity of knowing the world's affliction redemptively, that is, in a life-giving way (*Letters*, 137). She reflected on her years of experience as a factory worker:

> The combination of personal experience and sympathy for the wretched mass of people around me, in which I formed, even in my own eyes, an undistinguishable item, implanted so deep in my heart the affliction of social degradation that I have felt a slave ever since, in the Roman sense of the word. (*Letters*, 140)

In a 1942 letter to Maurice Schumann from New York, she indicated that her solidarity with afflicted people had reached the point of an obsession with the world's affliction during war (*Letters*, 156).

In a 1943 letter to her parents, she remarked that those who suffer the lowest degree of humiliation because they are deprived of social consideration and of reason itself are the only ones capable of telling the truth (*Letters*, 201). She also claimed that affliction is inarticulate, that afflicted people can only ask: "Why am I being hurt?" (*Essays*, 24). She identified with Christ on the cross as afflicted since he, too, asks that question (*Essays*, 10; *Letters*, 103). She concluded:

> Only by the supernatural working of grace can a soul pass through its own annihilation to the place where alone it can get the sort of attention which can attend to truth and to affliction. It is the same attention which listens to both of them. The name of this intense, pure, disinterested, gratuitous, generous attention is love. (*Essays*, 28)

Simone's experience in the factory and on a farm enabled her to write of the possibilities of France's regeneration, as requested of her by the Free French in London in 1943, the last year of her life. Her section on the uprootedness in the towns, *le déracinement ouvrier*, listed some of the woes of workers that lead to their sense of affliction, woes that she had herself experienced working in factories.[8] In her section on uprootedness in the countryside, *le déracinement paysan*, she noted: "When misfortune, *malheur*, bites too deeply, it creates a disposition toward misfortune, which makes people plunge headlong into it themselves, dragging others along with them" (*Roots*, 97).

Simone Weil's empathy with suffering people was so great that she had to deny herself what others could not have. When she was five years old, she stopped eating sugar since the soldiers at the front did not have access to it. When she began teaching at Le Puy, she would not eat more than the rations of those on relief and gave her surplus food to hungry people. In this context, it is understandable that she restricted her diet in England to what her people in France could eat on ration, and so died of malnutrition (*Waiting*, 14, 18, 34).

Her inability to enjoy what those less fortunate were denied was a factor in her refusal of baptism, as well as her need to identify with unbelievers, her sense of herself as an exile and an outsider in every human circle, her conviction that depriving herself of the sacraments she desired could be a purer contact than participation (*Waiting*, 48, 54–55). Her notion of redemptive suffering was rooted in identification with God's self-emptying in Christ. Our self-emptying involves the acceptance of suffering, viewed not as a punishment from God but rather as an opportunity to rely more on the God who wants to liberate us from pain. From this perspective, her image of God was not that of an angry tyrant forcing us to suffer in order to expiate or pay for the sins of the world. Rather she experienced God emptied and become other in Christ. Through a gradual process of self-purification, we are emptied in Christ. This kenotic spirituality has solid biblical and mystical roots in the Western Christian tradition, particularly in the lives and writings of Francis of Assisi and John of the Cross, to whom Weil often referred.[9]

Respect for the Dignity of the Worker:
A Spirituality of Work

For Simone Weil, the dignity of the worker was the basis for a spirituality of work. Throughout her life, Simone was preoccupied with the issue of oppression. She viewed it as a form of slavery that prevented human freedom. At the same time, she stood in solidarity with oppressed people. She saw a spirituality of work as a solution to the problem of oppression.

After having observed that humankind has already been subjected to military and economic oppression, she asked in 1933 whether we were suffering a new form of oppression exercised in the name of industrialization whereby the collective industrial machine was subordinating the individual.[10] She saw industrialization as a cause of the physical and moral wretchedness of the masses. She wanted the revolution to end social oppression, but she realized that industry reduces workers to be instruments of their employers.

For Weil, thought and action keep us from accepting servitude. That is to say, pain and failure can make us unhappy without humiliating us, as long as we dispose our own capacity for action. But we become slaves if all our movements proceed from a source other than our mind. We need to adapt our efforts to the piece of work being produced and coordinate with the efforts of our co-workers, thus retaining the use of our reason.[11]

Her respect for the dignity of the laborer underlay her respect for the dignity of labor. It was the basis of her spirituality of work, which she considered key to the true greatness of a civilization. She was aware of the negative and positive value of work. She called it a daily death because it does violence to human nature through exhaustion, preoccupation, monotony, and the weight of time.

She identified with the lowest class in the factory, women who were unskilled workers. She began to understand how they might act out their feelings of annoyance and frustration at home, since they could not express these feelings at work. But she did not articulate their plight in any overt form.[12]

She considered consent to the law of work, however, as the most perfect act of obedience. Thus all other human activities have less spiritual significance than physical labor. For this reason, physical labor should be the spiritual core of a well-ordered social life. Notice that she grounded her respect for the dignity of labor in her respect for the dignity of the laborer's consent to work. She emphasized the con-

scious relationship of the worker with matter and the minimizing of
mass production and passivity. She called contemplation the spiritual
function of physical labor. In other words, manual labor willingly con-
sented to can free us to live in the presence of God and to find God in
all things. By labor, the worker becomes the flesh of Christ given for
others.[13]

Struggle for Peace: A Mission of Social Justice

Simone Weil's struggle for international peace was a mission of social
justice. Her reflections on war reveal her changing attitudes during
the years 1933–43 in Europe when she went back and forth between
supporting armed revolution and supporting pacifism.

Weil began as a revolutionary. In 1933, she was opposed to absolute
pacifism and its condemnation of the use of violence and willing to see
the nuances of each war's purposes and process. But after her brief
experience of serving in a militia unit during the Spanish civil war, she
admitted her disillusionment. Revolution, especially in the form of civil
war, does not imply clear consciousness of a social problem.

She connected industrialism and capitalism with militarism. Today
we would add sexism, racism, and classism. For her, arms were a sign
of privilege, instruments of power along with machines, gold, and tech-
nical secrets. She perceived that in the race for power a form of slavery
ensued. She also saw how war and the search for wealth and production
substituted means for ends. She observed how the exercise of military
power multiplied wars and mobilized industrial activity. She concluded
that the focus ought to be not on the product of work but rather on the
worker as the highest value. "Industrial slavery" cannot produce free
workers; "military slavery" leads only to tyranny.[14] She observed that
the arms race demands the sacrifice of people to industrial productivity.

She published an article in 1936 presenting her absolute pacifism in
her dread of a world war, asking whether any war can bring more liberty, justice, or well-being to the world. In an essay defending France's
policy of neutrality in the Spanish civil war as a way of avoiding a
European war, she went so far as to call its opposite the policy of mutual assistance. In 1938, she rationalized her preference for what she
considered a lesser evil, German domination of Czechoslovakia, over
the greater evil of a war in Europe. This preference was embodied for
her in the signing of the Munich agreement on September 30, 1938.

Yet in 1939, Weil conceded that the condition of war was a possibility for liberation from tyranny. Despite her pacifist inclinations, she decided to work for Hitler's destruction the day he entered Prague in May 1939.[15]

Her concern that war be a means of liberation and not a means of reinforcing oppressive structures of power led her to conceive several personal plans. During the Germans' brutal suppression of a student uprising in Prague at the beginning of World War II, she presented a plan to parachute arms and volunteers, including herself, into Czechoslovakia to support the people's resistance, but the French political leaders turned it down. Then the French and American governments both rejected her idea of a corps of front-line nurses, herself among them. And the Free French in London refused her request to be parachuted into France as a saboteur or liaison person between the French living under the Occupation and the Free French headquarters in London (*Writings*, 234–35).

Simone Weil observed how the allied nations, particularly the United States, promised Europe peace through the use of guns. She claimed that the true mission of the French movement in London was above all a spiritual one of directing conscience on a national plane. Less than a month before her death, she wrote a letter explaining her decision to resign from the Free French movement. She named four obstacles that hindered her country from becoming a great civilization: a false conception of greatness, a degraded sense of justice, the idolization of money, and the lack of religious inspiration.[16]

The question that was paramount to her in working out her apparently inconsistent positions on war and peace was the immediate effect of war on the working classes: would war alleviate this oppression or reinforce it? In writing about the possibilities of an economic boycott of Hitler's Germany, she urged that gestures of international solidarity be made against the tortures being inflicted on German workers (*Writings*, 229, 250).

She claimed that Christ called love of one's neighbor justice (*Waiting*, 139). Our right relationship with others implies our acceptance of them as they are and our willingness to change oppressive structures in order to assure their rights. Her struggle for peace was a mission of social justice, which called her to unmask forms of oppression by siding with the oppressed and challenging the oppressor.

Attention: Openness to Experience the Sacred

Simone Weil had a rare capacity for attention that she considered a special openness to experience the sacred, that is, the transcendent mystery at the heart of our lives. It was the source of her peace within herself and with God.

Her spiritual quest did not always include a quest for a particular religion. In her travels through Europe, she often went to Roman Catholic services in order to hear Gregorian chant (*Letters*, 80–81, 87). Hearing fishermen's wives singing in procession honoring Our Lady of Sorrows in a Portuguese village convinced her that Christianity is the religion of slaves. She meant this in the positive sense of a slave's attentiveness to the master and ability to wait, not in the negative sense of the slave's unwillingness to obey and inability to revolt.

In 1937, she went to a chapel in Assisi and felt compelled to kneel down in the presence of the sacred. The following year, she spent Holy Week with her mother at the Benedictine Abbey of Solesmes, and while letting go of the pain of her migraine headaches in order to hear the chanting, she understood that it was possible to love God in affliction. By this, she did not mean to make pain an end in itself. Reciting George Herbert's poem "Love" to herself, she experienced Christ taking possession of her for the first time, and realized then that it was not only a beautiful poem but a prayer. She felt his real presence. She and Gustave Thibon had agreed to memorize the Lord's Prayer in Greek. Out in the fields, she used to recite it to herself with attention, and sometimes on these occasions she experienced Christ's presence to her.[17]

In 1943, she posited that what is sacred in us is what is nonpersonal in us. She pointed out that Gregorian chant, Romanesque architecture, the invention of geometry, and the *Iliad* were not meant to reveal the personality. She concluded that truth and beauty are nonpersonal and anonymous (*Essays*, 13).

Her notion of God as impersonal was not a nihilistic notion of a dead God whose self-emptying implies removal from the world and from life. Rather it was a positive insight that relativized feminine and masculine metaphors for God; it respected the nuances of symbolic language and recognized the mystery of God's presence in the world and in life.[18]

I believe it was her constant practice of attention, *l'attention*, that opened her to experience the sacred. In 1937, Weil wrote: "To become conscious of even the simplest realities one needs to pay attention" (*Essays*, 150). In her 1942 letter to Joë Bousquet, she admitted that due to the pain in her nervous system, she had struggled for ten years to make the effort of attention and intellectual work: "I was sustained by the faith, which I acquired at the age of fourteen, that no true effort of attention is ever wasted, even though it may never have any visible result, either direct or indirect."[19] In a letter to Maurice Schumann, she wrote of the value of creative attention (*Letters*, 175). This creative attention is an openness to creative intuition. In her notebooks, she observed that the value of solitude lies in its superior potential for attention (*Notebooks*, 12).

Weil is a spiritual guide for us today by her attention to the secular. It came innately to her to integrate the secular and faith.

Attention, for her, was the attitude of heart that best prepares us for prayer. She encouraged students to develop the faculty of attention as they worked on geometry problems and Latin exercises, since the habit of attention is the substance of prayer. What did she mean by attention? "Attention consists of suspending our thought, leaving it detached, empty, and ready to be penetrated by the object" (*Waiting*, 111). It involves both attentiveness and waiting. She claimed that the first duty of a school is to develop in students the faculty of attention.[20]

She wrote: "Attention, taken to its highest degree, is prayer. It presupposes faith and love" (*Notebooks*, 205). And she described the relationship between studies and prayer:

> Since prayer is but attention in its pure form, and since studies constitute a gymnastic of the attention, it follows that every school exercise should be a refraction of spiritual life. But this depends on the use of a method. A certain way of doing a Latin translation, a certain way of doing a problem in geometry — and not just any sort of way — these constitute a gymnastic of the attention calculated to render it more fitted for prayer. (*Notebooks*, 597)

She wrote in her journal: "Absolutely unmixed attention is prayer" (*Grace*, 106). She connected attention with the rigor of clear thinking and the honest search for truth when she wrote: "In the intellectual order, the virtue of humility is nothing more nor less than the power of attention" (*Grace*, 116).

Simone referred again and again to attention. She urged us to keep our attention fixed on the truth that even though we want something to live for, there is nothing in *this* world for which to live. She observed that if we say the Lord's Prayer or contemplate Christ in the Blessed

Sacrament with the fullest attention of which we are capable, we can be certain of being delivered from some of the evil within us (*Love*, 148-49).

Attention, *l'attention*, is an active receptivity that opens us to experience the sacred.

Waiting for God: Obedience to the Truth

A fifth attitude of heart that Simone Weil lived and wrote about is waiting, *l'attente*, for God, which was for her a form of obedience to the truth. She invited us to let go, stay motionless, wait without trying to know what we await, knowing for certain that God will come to us (*Love*, 159).

She observed that God comes in God's own time, like a beggar free to keep coming back or not. Our consent to God is a sacred thing and is as essential to obedience as to love. Through our consent, God sows a seed in us, and from that moment our part is only to wait and not regret the consent we have given, the mystical Yes. By our consent to love we come to belong to God and to allow the love of God to pass through us, since "God alone is capable of loving God" (*Love*, 181).[21] She described objects of the implicit love of God: religious ceremonies, the beauty and order of the world, and our neighbor (*Waiting*, 137-215).[22]

Attention and waiting are linked together. "They will bear fruit in attentive patience (to attend — to bear a shock)" (*FLN*, 82), she wrote, and later on added: "Waiting patiently in expectation is the foundation of the spiritual life" (*FLN*, 99). She called this waiting in patience the attitude of the slave, ready for any order from the master, or for no order, claiming that humility is attentive patience (*Pensées*, 144-45; *FLN*, 110-11). This kind of hope enables one to wait indefinitely without budging in patience, *en hypomoné*.[23]

Her choice of the way of obedience even to the Cross was her response to the truth of her own being, her insistence on personal integrity. She knew intuitively that she was not called to be baptized. She gave Father Perrin, her confidant and friend, various reasons in the course of their correspondence, but uppermost was her obedience to God's will, her need to be herself and to honor what she most deeply wanted and was (*Waiting*, 47). Honoring herself was her way of reverencing God.

An aspect of this obedience to the truth of her being was her intellectual honesty. Part of her struggle about being baptized was between her attraction to the mystical and sacramental dimensions of Christianity, and her resistance to certain institutional elements in Catholicism. We could learn from her in this regard. She recognized that baptism symbolizes and satisfies the desire for new birth, but she thought that it should not involve submitting to the social organization of the church. Nor should it be withheld due to social conditions (*FLN*, 224–25, 288–89, 298). She could not support the institutional church's discouragement of intellectual honesty in matters of faith, by its use of the formula of condemnation *anathema sit*, its acceptance of the Old Testament conception of a warrior God, its denial of the implicit presence of Christ in non-Christian religions, its suspicion of a scientific conception of the world with which it had to reconcile such mysteries of the faith as creation, providence, and miracles, and its difficulty in allowing critical dissent and religious freedom.[24]

Simone sometimes used spousal metaphors to describe intimacy with God. She used the spousal metaphor for waiting:

Our love for God should be like a woman's love for a man, which dares not express itself by making advances but consists only in waiting. God is the Bridegroom, and it is for the bridegroom to come to the one he has chosen and speak to her and lead her away. The bride-to-be should only wait. (*Love*, 157)

She returned to this analogy in talking about our turning to God through the transforming power of suffering and of joy:

When either of them comes to us we have to open the very center of our soul to it, as a woman opens her door to messengers from her beloved. What does it matter to a lover if the messenger is courteous or rough so long as he gives her a message? (*Love*, 181)

She used bridal imagery when she described the effort that brings a person to salvation: she contrasted the effort of looking or of listening, the effort of receptive attention and consent whereby a fiancée accepts her lover, with the muscular effort of the will. She claimed that we do not search for God unless bidden: "The role of the future wife is to wait.... To long for God and to renounce all the rest, that alone can save us."[25] Her use of the spousal imagery can help us grasp what she meant by waiting for God; we are, however, aware of the potential danger in using such language since it does not describe the mutuality characteristic of many marriages today.

Waiting, *l'attente*, for God is a receptivity like that of a slave and of a lover. It is a form of obedience to the truth. One can say that Weil's entire life was a search for the truth.[26]

Conclusion

Simone Weil witnessed with her life to a solidarity with afflicted people, allowing herself to experience the plight of poor people and denying herself what the least privileged could not enjoy. She respected the dignity of the worker and was asked toward the end of her life to write a long memorandum on the rights and duties of the state and the individual. She worked hard for social justice: picketing with workers at Le Puy, writing about the inhuman conditions of factory workers that she had herself suffered firsthand, fighting in the Spanish civil war, and then doing what she could in England to help the people of occupied France during World War II. She was attentive to the present moment and to the presence of the sacred. Her waiting for God made her obedient to the truth of her being.

Simone Weil was called by God to lay down her life for others whom she would never know, to suffer redemptively on behalf of others. It is significant in this regard that she took a year off from her teaching, lived the life of an unskilled factory worker, and saw the humiliation and affliction of her fellow workers. It is also significant that during World War II, she was not content to stay safe with her parents in the United States. She found a way to get as far as England, willing to help serve the people of her country as a writer, as a front-line nurse, or on a liaison mission. And finally, it is significant that during her time in England she could not bear to eat more than what had been rationed for people in occupied France. At the same time, she felt uncomfortable eating any food when she was not contributing to the British war effort. This practice endangered her health and eventually led to her death, since she refused nutrition at the sanitarium. On this point, we need to ask whether she went too far in identifying with those less fortunate than herself.

One might argue that she was suicidal in this behavior, but "it is only suicidal in the sense that it is suicidal to refuse to get into a lifeboat in order to leave more room for others."[27] She herself condemned suicide (*Notebooks*, 1, 262). One wonders whether she actually died of anorexia nervosa.[28] For some deeply spiritual people, there is at times a fine line between an asceticism of self-denial and anorexia nervosa. One plays on the other. Weil was led by her own asceticism and mysticism of solidarity with afflicted people to live and die as they did, one of them as well as one with them.[29]

To understand Simone Weil, one needs to understand her call to self-deprivation, to an asceticism from which most shrink. She deprived herself of food in order to be closer to the hungry. She deprived herself of her teaching position for a year to be closer to workers by sharing their life. She deprived herself of baptism in order to be closer to unbelievers. It is denial at one level for deeper identification at another level. She was so convinced of the life-giving power of deprivation that she could write that she envied the crucifixion of Christ (*Waiting*, 83).

Perhaps it was her propensity for self-denial that led her to deprive herself of institutional Christianity in order to be closer to mystical Christianity. Her attraction to self-deprivation was based on her experiential insight into redemptive suffering. She believed that by denying oneself, one can establish someone else by creative affirmation (*Waiting*, 147–48).

Her 1940–43 notebooks reveal her preoccupation with Christ's redemptive passion, disgrace, isolation, loneliness, and anguish on the cross. His acceptance of his affliction helped to open him to the love of God (*Notebooks*, 25, 27).[30] Can one say that knowingly or unknowingly she took upon herself the condition of a slave in identification with Christ, first as a factory worker then as imprudently malnourished in England? It is possible to assert that Simone Weil lived a spirituality of the pierced heart: she was conscious of identifying with Christ and with other people in their pain as well as their joy, in their affliction and in their experience of the love of God.[31]

She used experience as her point of departure. Unwilling to teach philosophy in an abstract way, she grounded her metaphysics in her work in the factories and fields. Her frequent articles about workers' rights and responsibilities must be understood in light of her active participation. Only when she realized she could love God in affliction did she reflect on this possibility in print.

Simone Weil's mystical experiences did not remove her from political involvement but intensified it. For her, God was not the God of institutionalized religion but the God of truth out of whose self-emptying came creation, the Incarnation, and the passion of Christ. Her insight into the passion of Christ, the afflicted one, motivated her to continue to work for the liberation of afflicted people. She continued to wait for

God at her desk, on the battlefield, and finally on her hospital bed. In this way, she lived a spirituality of work that is relevant for us today as we explore the socio-political dimensions of a mysticism of everyday faith. This spirituality recognizes that while suffering is not to be sought, it is to be accepted and can have benefits for others even as it empties us of ourselves. This spirituality also recognizes that we are called to build the earth and care for everything in it and at the same time to wait for God to act.[32] Weil broke ground for an insistence on the political dimension of contemporary spirituality.[33]

Her integrity led her to distinguish the mystical and institutional dimensions of Catholicism. Her intellectual honesty forced her to resist another level of oppression, a subtle intellectual oppression imposed by the Catholic Church in her day and ours. She favored many of the objections for which Modernism was condemned and which only Vatican II has taken seriously, for example, the church's resistance to an evolutionary worldview. She was able to tolerate a great deal of ambiguity and alienation, to live on the threshold of the church, to welcome God the beggar at her doorstep, to die outside her country, to eat like and work for her people, to wait for God like a slave, to struggle for peace and justice in solidarity with all afflicted people.

Simone Weil can be a spiritual guide for us today. She turns our gaze from the comfortable lifestyle of the affluent to the plight of the afflicted. She directs our focus not to big business but to the factory workers and farmers who are exploited by industrialism. Her struggle for international peace reveals the political dimension of her spirituality. Her conviction that attention opens us to the sacred in the present moment can strengthen our own capacity for attention. For her, waiting for God is a humble stance before God. It enables us to listen to the truth of our being and to the reality around us.

Weil challenges us to do the deed of love. Haunted by her vision of a better world for all, she was not content to teach philosophy to high school girls. She felt impelled to take a radical step to identify with workers. Not only did she write articles supporting their rights; she also became one of them and one with them by joining workers' unions. Her concern about the oppressive conditions of workers colored her changing views about war and peace. What was uppermost to her was what would help the workers. She was, in this sense, a prophet of "liberationist spirituality."[34]

Weil inspires us to open our hearts to God. For her, attention unifies our sense impressions and makes us mindful of the present moment.

For her, too, Eastern religions like Buddhism foster mindfulness and meditation through breathing exercises and yoga.[35] Waiting in patience is also the active receptivity that frees us to receive the surprise gift of God's presence.

Weil seemed to accept suffering in faith. She claimed to have experienced Christ's presence during migraine headaches. She perceived that Christ could still love God even in his afflicted state on the cross. This experience and insight helped her see the relationship between the love of God and suffering. She suffered a great deal in her life and found a God-meaning in this pain. To our North American culture, which is afraid of suffering, she offers the hope that in pain we can find meaning if not relief. Her sensitivity to the social degradation involved in affliction can deepen and renew our compassion for AIDS victims, unwed mothers, rape victims, and homeless women. She shows us that solidarity with afflicted people can become our way to truth and can lead us to wisdom.

Her ambivalence about institutional membership had to do with several factors: her high standards and strong set of values that she saw espoused, however imperfectly, by certain organizations like the Roman Catholic Church and the Free French in London, her disillusionment in face of the gap between the ideal and the reality lived, her propensity to be unallied with any one group, and her desire to build communion with others. Although she held intellectual disagreements with some church beliefs, her choice not to be baptized came rather from an asceticism to identify with the impoverished and from her solidarity with unbelievers. At the end of her life, she persisted in eating a war-ration diet in her solidarity with her people in occupied France even though her tuberculosis required eating to recover. Her choice, indeed, challenges our way of meeting our basic hunger for God and for social justice.

READINGS

Waiting for God (San Francisco: Harper & Row, 1951) is a collection of Simone Weil's correspondence with Father Perrin and four of her essays, including a first version of "The Love of God and Affliction." *Gravity and Grace* (New York: Routledge & Kegan Paul, Ark, 1987) is Gustave Thibon's collection of Weil's writings drawn from the personal manuscripts she confided to him. Three of her key essays, "Some Thoughts on the Love of God," "Some Reflections on the Love of God," and an extended version of "The Love of God and Affliction," appear in *On Science, Necessity, and the Love of God* (New York: Oxford University Press, 1968), and *Gateway to God* (Glasgow: William Collins Sons, Fontana, 1974). Her "Reflections concerning the Causes of Liberty and Social Oppression" is in *Oppression and Liberty* (London: Routledge & Kegan Paul, 1958). Her "Factory Journal" and reflections on war and peace are in *Formative Writings 1929–1941*, ed. and trans. Dorothy Tuck McFarland and Wilhelmina Van Ness (Amherst, Mass.: University of Massachusetts Press, 1987).

The standard biography is Simone Pétrement, *Simone Weil: A Life* (New York: Random House, Pantheon, 1976). Dorothy Tuck McFarland, *Simone Weil* (New York: Frederick Ungar, 1983) explores some problems in approaching Weil. A recent welcome addition is Gabriella Fiori, *Simone Weil: An Intellectual Biography* (Athens, Ga.: University of Georgia Press, 1989). In *Between the Human and the Divine: The Political Thought of Simone Weil* (Totowa, N.J.: Rowman and Littlefield, 1988), Mary G. Dietz cogently argues that Weil's work reflects her lifelong tension between the political and the spiritual.

Two outstanding studies that explore the potential relationship between Simone Weil's thought and contemporary feminist concerns are Lawrence A. Blum and Victor J. Seidler, *A Truer Liberty: Simone Weil and Marxism* (New York: Routledge, Chapman & Hall, 1989); and Thomas Idinopulos and Josephine Knopp, eds., *Mysticism, Nihilism, Feminism: New Critical Essays on the Theology of Simone Weil* (Johnson City, Tenn.: Institute of Social Sciences & Arts, 1984). On her solidarity with the afflicted, see Eric O. Springsted, *Simone Weil and the Suffering of Love* (Cambridge, Mass.: Cowley, 1986).

5
THOMAS MERTON

(1915–1968)

A Living Mystery of Solitude

T HOMAS MERTON would seem to be one of those rare persons who let himself be guided by the Holy Spirit acting directly through interior movements and indirectly through other people. Merton's childhood years of loneliness had a formative effect with respect to the development of gifts. Loneliness was gradually transformed into solitude as Merton let himself be guided by his own search for the meaning and purpose of life, his own search for God. His hunger for human intimacy was outdone only by his hunger for intimacy with God. And solitude was the key leading him to a monastic life of contemplation and compassion.

He became a spiritual guide for the Trappist scholastics and novices, even for an anonymous public for whom he wrote books, and for the many people with whom he communicated in person and in letters. Merton was vitally in touch with his own experience of God, with the story of Jesus written into his life. Part of his growth as a spiritual guide springs from his innate attentiveness to the movements of the Spirit in his own life. Spiritual growth was also fostered through his careful reading of and reflection upon the writings of spiritual guides in different traditions. Another factor in his maturing process was the impact of solitude on his prayer and thought, especially at the hermitage where he spent the last years of his life. What characterized this development? What was important to Merton?

In a world afraid of loneliness, Merton challenged us to re-examine the perennial value of solitude. To North American society marked by low self-esteem, Merton spoke of self-acceptance. To those more comfortable learning new ways to pray, he connected spiritual direction with a process of becoming free to be oneself in God. To people who are victims and perpetrators of violence at many levels, he kept using peace as a touchstone of authentically human decision-making. To those who pray often, who may have disassociated their prayer from their lives, he wrote of contemplation in a world of action.

In this chapter, I elaborate on aspects of the spiritual life based on Merton's lived experience: solitude as necessity, self-acceptance as integration, spiritual direction as growth in interior freedom, peace as touchstone, and contemplation as seeking God's will and finding God's mercy.

Solitude as Necessity: A Way to Compassion

One of Merton's convictions was his insistence that solitude is not a luxury but a necessity. He was drawn not to an active apostolate, but to monasticism, a way of life through which loneliness is slowly transformed into solitude by the power of the Spirit. Merton often associated solitude with Mary, the Mother of God, calling her Our Lady of Solitude. For years he anguished over whether to choose a more austere form of monastic solitude by joining the Carthusians, but he was dissuaded from doing so by his superiors. One of his lifelong struggles was trying to integrate his vocation to be a monk with his vocation to be a writer, both solitary occupations. His first abbot, Dom Frederic, welcomed his talents for writing and ordered him under obedience to write. Merton continued to write poems and books about Roman Catholicism, spirituality, and his life as a Trappist monk.[1]

He concentrated on his desire for solitude in *The Sign of Jonas*, which described his priestly ordination. He called poverty a function of solitude and claimed that rejoicing in our imperfections is the only way to true solitude. He talked about taking time to be alone for prolonged prayer. He wrote forcefully of the essence of a solitary vocation as being a vocation to fear, helplessness, isolation in the invisible God. He then went on to write about the relationship between solitude and dependence on God, emptiness, silence, love, and the solitude of God. In writing of the necessity of silence, he distinguished inner and outer silence. He ended by relating solitude to compassion, in particular, to Christ's compassion, for example, the way Jesus was strengthened in solitude to nourish and respond to others, to the hungry crowd who came to hear him speak.[2]

In solitude, Merton experienced the nightwatch that he described

in the epilogue to *The Sign of Jonas;* it was for him an experience of
the divine speaking through icons on the novitiate walls. In solitude
he experienced the nightwatch described a decade later in *Conjectures,*
which was for him an experience of the divine speaking through the
humanity of the novices entrusted to him.[3]

Toward the end of his life, he kept asking for and finally got permission to live in a hermitage on the monastery grounds. He went to
this hermitage to be, to be himself, to live as God wanted him to live
with his love of God and of people, with his strengths and weaknesses.
This hermitage was, I think, a symbol of who Merton really was, since
he was most himself alone before God. He would be there a few hours
before the solitude would again bring him back to his own center, to the
truth of his being. Here he felt that his life as a writer and his life as
a monk were integrated in this little house that held his rows of books
and witnessed his hours of listening to God. Notice he did not seek
solitude to escape, but to find community and communion at a deeper
level.

In *Conjectures of a Guilty Bystander,* Merton is adamant that solitude is to be preserved as a necessity, not a luxury. To be true to ourselves,
we must say no since people are constantly trying to use us to help
them foster the illusions by which they live (*Conjectures,* 96–97). I wonder here if Merton is perhaps talking to himself. In fact, I would call
this freedom for solitude his metaphor of the interior life, his image of
contemplation, his notion of interiority. In her biography of Merton,
Monica Furlong calls solitude "a form of essential nutrition to him."[4]
Another image of interiority that he uses is the French expression *le
point vierge,* literally, the virgin point. *Le point vierge* is, for Merton,
that point of our dependence on God which is deeper than our desires
and freer than our fantasies.[5] I wonder if *le point vierge* is Merton's
principle of unity in interpreting his own life journey to God. Merton
has been a powerful spiritual guide for many through his insights into
the value of solitude and surrender.

He described his sense of identity in terms of solitude: "My task is
only to be what I am, a man seeking God in silence and solitude, with
deep respect for the demands and realities of his own vocation, and fully
aware that others too are seeking the truth in their own way" (*Action,*
245). And from his ongoing conversion to solitude came his sense of
mission: "My own peculiar task in my Church and in my world has
been that of the solitary explorer who, instead of jumping on all the
latest bandwagons at once, is bound to search the existential depths of

faith in its silence, its ambiguities, and in those certainties which lie deeper than the bottom of anxiety."[6]

Merton's involvement with the world sprang from his own solitude. In his monastic spirituality, the essential factor was solitude: "It is clear to me that solitude is my vocation, not as a flight from the world — but as my place in the world" (*Jonas*, 251). This solitude was not a protection from the world's concerns but rather a way to compassion: "True solitude is deeply aware of the world's needs. It does not hold the world at arm's length" (*Conjectures*, 10). After twenty years as a monk, he learned to view the world with greater compassion, "seeing those in it not as alien to myself, not as particular and deluded strangers, but as identified with myself."[7]

Self-Acceptance as Integration: A Way to the Real Self

For whatever reasons, Merton's growth in self-acceptance was a lifelong struggle. Moments of self-acceptance were therapeutic and freeing for him as they are for each of us. He was a man with a high need for both independence and interdependence. Abbot John Eudes Bamberger understood that Merton was not cut out to be a full-time hermit.[8] Rather, his own need to love and be loved concretely kept him relating to the world and to his fellow monks. It is a question whether he might have done better to go for longer stretches to the hermitage, and at other times to keep more consistent contact with the monastic community. Merton had to come to grips with the dichotomy in his life between living a monk in the abstract and in the concrete, between emotional maturity and emotional adolescence, and between the ideal self and the actual self.[9]

Merton's life has been described a number of ways. He called his own life story *The Seven Storey Mountain*. Michael Mott called it *The Seven Mountains of Thomas Merton*.[10] Merton called a segment of his monastic journals *The Sign of Jonas*. The whale represents the solitude in which he came to discover and accept his monastic identity. Merton identified with Jonas who also avoided his vocation for a long time (*Jonas*, 329–30, 351–52).

Merton was a complex man with a humble openness to growth. He made some serious mistakes in his life but let them become learning experiences, opportunities for reflection and improvement. When he was a university student at Cambridge, England, he fathered a child illegitimately and realized years later how little he had integrated his needs for intimacy with his sexuality.[11] This same issue surfaced again in the last years of his life when he fell in love with a nurse at a hospital in Louisville and realized painfully that he still had to go through stages of his own emotional adolescence.[12] His hunger for human intimacy seems to have been outdone only by his hunger for intimacy with God.

Since Merton's own early life was marked by religious experience rather than by practices of piety, it is understandable that his monastic life was also characterized by a quest for the experience of God rather than a preoccupation with ritual. One finds this singleminded concentration in both editions of *Seeds of Contemplation*.

His readings in desert spirituality, psychology, and Eastern spirituality led him to focus on the distinction between the false self and the true self, a theme of his book *The New Man*.[13] Using Jacques Maritain's distinction between the individual and the person, Merton wrote of letting go of the false self in search of the true self.[14] Later in "The Inner Experience," he distinguished between the compulsive exterior self and the spontaneous inner self.[15] In *New Seeds of Contemplation*, Merton expanded the last chapter of *Seeds of Contemplation* with a discussion of the inner and external self. Painfully aware of his alienated, individualistic external self, Merton led a life of prayer as a way to the awakening of the inner self, a way to integration.[16] Merton recognized that the ability to accept oneself is the ability to accept others, the world, and God.

In *Conjectures of a Guilty Bystander*, Merton writes that the actual Christian task is "accepting ourselves as we are in our confusion, infidelity, disruption, ferment, and even desperation" (*Conjectures*, 71). He wrote this in the context of reflecting on the breakdown of Western culture and the problem of racism. Hence he was writing not only about individual self-acceptance but corporate, ethnic, national, global self-acceptance.

Part of his task of self-acceptance was a growing understanding of the world. When he first became a monk, he consciously rejected the world; twenty years later, he was drawn to accept the world, to become one with its pain and poverty before God. This coming to terms with the world allowed him to integrate the sacred and the secular and to adopt an incarnational approach, seeing Christ in others, the beauty of God in the depths of the person (*Conjectures*, 156-58). It enabled him to experience his connectedness with all that is.

He also needed to accept his incompleteness and imperfection, letting go of the task of personal growth and staying open to the gift of integration, the gift of the Spirit.[17] He was very concerned about the growth of one's real self and this self he called Christ. In a letter to Dr. Daisetz Suzuki, world-renowned for his writings on Zen Buddhism, he writes: "The Christ we seek is within us, in our inmost self, *is* our inmost self, and yet infinitely transcends ourselves. We have to be 'found in him' and yet be perfectly ourselves and free from the domination of any image of him other than himself."[18] His growth in self-acceptance led him to integration and the experience of his real self.

Spiritual Direction as Growth in Interior Freedom: A Way to Union with God

Merton allowed spiritual writers and theologians like Pope John XXIII and Karl Rahner, S.J., to be his spiritual guides in facilitating his conversion to a twentieth-century Christian commitment to the world. He, in turn, became a spiritual director not only to the Trappist novices and scholastics who were entrusted to him, but also, through his writings, to many people. For example, in *Life and Holiness*, he wrote about such relevant themes as the social perspectives of charity, the intrinsic value of work, and the importance of human dignity in a secular society.[19] As Elena Malits has observed, autobiographical writing was part of his spiritual guidance of himself and of his many readers.[20]

In his little book called *Spiritual Direction and Meditation*, Merton described what he meant by spiritual direction. He called it a continuous process of formation and guidance, in which we Christians are led and encouraged in our special vocation, so that, by faithful correspondence to the graces of the Holy Spirit, we may attain to the particular end of our vocation and to union with God. It is spiritual guidance, not merely ethical, social, or psychological help. The function of the spiritual guide is to focus on the life of the whole person, not merely the life of the mind or of the heart. According to Merton, the purpose of spiritual direction is to penetrate beneath the surface of our lives, to get behind the persona that we present to the world, and to evoke our inner freedom and truth, which is the likeness of Christ in us. Part of this person's function is to help others discern the movements of the spirits, to help them sort out which inspirations come from the spirit of evil and which from the Holy Spirit. Another part of this function is to enable another to recognize and follow the inspirations of the Holy Spirit in everyday life. A spiritual guide creates an informal, trusting atmosphere in which a person can feel known and understood. As spiritual guides, we cannot give to others what we do not ourselves possess. Spiritual direction is necessarily personal. It enables the director to encounter our real self and our false self. Such candid and profound self-revelation is only possible in an atmosphere that evokes it.[21]

One can see Thomas Merton as spiritual guide at work in his essays on meditation. He began by describing meditation as unitive and loving knowledge. Its distinctive characteristic is that it is a search for truth springing from love and seeking to possess the truth by love as well as by knowledge. Merton cautioned that in our eagerness to become "mystics," we can take our prayer too seriously. A contemplative, on the other hand, is for him "one who takes God seriously, who is famished for truth, who seeks to live in generous simplicity, in the spirit" (*Direction*, 33). A good spiritual guide can balance excessive asceticism, not with an overdose of sociability but rather with the simplicity and satisfaction of an ordinary life lived at a humane pace (*Direction*, 36).

He also noted the difficulty of integrating emotions into our life of prayer. Some find that their prayer is dry and seems to bear no fruit, so they give up. Others are always emoting in prayer and then start equating its success with the intensity of their feelings. Both are extremes to be avoided since the atmosphere of meditation is peaceful. Merton enumerated certain basic helps: ongoing recollection during the day, a sense of our poverty in God's sight, leisurely times of transition between work and formal prayer, sincerity, concentrating the interior life on union with God, a careful choice of a subject for prayer. He listed the essentials of meditative prayer as a sincere effort at recollection, the attempt to focus on what we are meditating about, the desire to live what we come to see, and communion. He concluded by describing meditation as awakening our interior self and attuning ourselves inwardly to the Holy Spirit (*Direction*, 43-99).

Merton insisted on the necessity of spiritual direction for those trying to deepen their life of prayer as a way of helping us discern the movements of the Spirit and as a way of cutting through our blindness. He pointed out how this task differs from that of the therapist, who helps us analyze the roots of our behavior and the projections in our relationships. It differs also from that of the pastoral counselor, who helps us integrate our relationship with ourselves, others, and God. The spiritual guide is interested primarily in helping us deepen and develop our relationship with God.

Out of his struggle, Merton had a wonderful empathy with others struggling with their identity. He seemed, if you will, scandal-proof. Ernesto Cardenal, a former novice under Merton who later founded a Christian lay community in Nicaragua called Solentiname, witnesses to this empathy. When Cardenal as a novice would come to Merton for spiritual direction, Merton would ask him about his country and poets and politics, everything that Cardenal thought he had to renounce. In this way, Merton gradually led him to accept all of his interests and concerns as parts of himself that were to be treasured and transformed for the glory of God and the service of others.[22]

Merton wrote essays on monastic renewal, many of which are on spiritual direction. For example, in "Final Integration: Toward a 'Monastic Therapy,'" he underlined the importance of existential anxiety as an invitation to growth and transformation. In this perspective, the spiritual guide facilitates a breakthrough that can lead to psychic rebirth and a transcultural identity (*Action*, 219–31).

For Merton, spiritual direction played a significant role in growth in interior freedom. He saw it as a way to union with God.[23]

Peace as Touchstone: A Way to Live the Truth

Merton looked for deep peace in himself and in others as the infallible sign of God's action and as a way of living the truth. In a 1941 letter to Robert Lax, perhaps his closest friend, he described his vocation to the Trappists in terms of seeking peace, of listening to and learning from peace.[24] Another example of how Merton considered peace a touchstone concerns his own brother John Paul. Merton helped to prepare him for baptism shortly before John Paul's death during World War II. Merton remarked that after his brother's baptism, John Paul looked quiet, happy, completely serene (*Seven*, 397–404).

Summoned by the draft board during World War II, Merton called himself a noncombatant objector since he denounced the immorality of war, although he was declared unfit for health reasons (*Seven*, 312). In the later years of his life, he worked prophetically for peace and justice in the world. He connected with Joan Baez, Dan Berrigan, S.J., Jim Forest, and others in the peace movement in the United States. He wrote books on the topic and was censured for writing what he circulated privately as his "Cold War Letters" and "Peace in the Post-Christian Era."

Thomas Merton offered his conjectures about violence and peace as "a guilty bystander." His book by that name marks a turning point in his own thinking about the ethical implications of contemplation. Even though he had chosen the silent life of a monk rather than the involved life of a social worker in Harlem, he reassessed his values in the 1960s and came to see that prayer and social action were not mutually exclusive but rather interdependent. His solitary existence, particularly in the hermitage, prevented him from engaging in certain possibilities for exchanges of thought about current issues and concerns in North America, but paved the way for his faith vision of peace to deepen and develop. A significant turning point for him was his growing acceptance of the world he had at one time rejected; he realized that as a monk he had made a special commitment to the world's progress. Behind this attitudinal shift was an integration in himself of the natural and the supernatural, due to such incidents as his 1948 and 1957 trips into Louisville and the process of documenting his U.S. citizenship in 1951. As James Baker wrote: "Contemplation is the key to Merton's social theory."[25]

Merton felt a genuine compassion for people and a concern for their rights and needs. Notice that here again peace is the touchstone of his experience. What is asked of him is not a rejection of the world but rather a response to Christ in the world, in the poor and oppressed, in the few people entrusted to him, and in unbelievers (*Conjectures*, 15).[26] Peace, then, becomes the touchstone of his experiences, a peace that is not an avoidance of the demands of everyday living, but rather the freedom to make a response, to take responsibility.

In the early 1960s, Merton wrote a series of significant and prophetic antiwar articles for the *Catholic Worker*, urging people to understand the psychological forces operative in themselves and in society. He predicted that we would be plagued by a war madness in the post-Christian era that could precipitate war while we claimed to maintain peace; he proposed that the root of war is fear, fear of self as well as fear of the enemy; and he urged a humble, realistic love.[27]

Merton recognized the enormity of national suicide and the dispar-ity between a nation simply defending itself when attacked and trying to annihilate its enemy, the inevitable result of nuclear weapons. Merton supported workers who participated in the peace strike of January 1962 and urged Christians to refuse to help make nuclear weapons. He saw that the cold war threat was creating a new ethic that tried to justify a nuclear war. Merton foresaw that when Christians reject their own ethics, they begin to promote war. He was overtly opposed to war "realists" who were willing to let war destroy Christian values, who blatantly were prepared to calculate "acceptable losses" and to anticipate the time when survivors would emerge from their shelters and take up their work again: the Christian ethic of love must be updated to deal not only with conventional weapons but also with nuclear arms. He held that Christians have a moral responsibility to protest global suicide; for example, it is not our choice to decide that millions of civilians should die rather than be communist.[28]

In 1964, he was admonished by his superiors not to write further about nuclear war, but at the same time he chided popes, bishops, and theologians for not condemning it.[29] Merton denounced Christians' "cold war religion," which could sanction a nuclear war with Russia as part of a Christian campaign against communism: relative pacifism can condone a just war but not a nuclear war.[30]

He urged a nonviolent resistance to war.[31] He saw that militarism and racism had similar roots. Living in a later decade, he might have connected them also with sexism and classism.[32]

In *Seeds of Destruction*, he wrote that his contemplative life as a monk was not a withdrawal from the world's sufferings: "The monastic flight from the world into the desert is not a mere refusal to know anything about the world, but a total rejection of all standards of judgment which imply attachment to a history of delusion, egoism and sin."[33] For this reason, he presented his positions not only as a monk but also as a responsible citizen. While he was clear that his call to solitude precluded direct political action, he was also clear that his life of contemplation issued in nonviolent resistance.

For Merton as for other contemporary spiritual guides, peace is not only a touchstone of God's action in our personal lives, but the gift of God offered to those who try to live a contemplative lifestyle, a lifestyle that cannot help urging us to search for justice. In the deep peace of contemplative prayer, his solitude was transformed into compassion.

Contemplation:
A Way to Mutual Interdependence

For Merton, contemplation has to do with seeking, finding, and doing God's will. One could say that every book he wrote is about contemplation because every book he wrote is about seeking, finding, and doing God's will. What he means by God's will is not an exterior command that goes against the grain, or a rote form of behavior. Rather God's will is intimately connected with the truth of our identity in God. We see this first in *The Seven Storey Mountain*, in which Merton traced his journey to God. In *The Sign of Jonas*, we are dealing with a different Merton, not the prodigal son who has squandered his fortune on wine, women, and song, but a serious monk preparing for ordination to priesthood. And what does this step mean to him? It means a contemplative experience of doing God's will: "My priestly ordination was, I felt, the one great secret for which I had been born" (*Jonas*, 181).

In *Seeds of Contemplation*, Merton used the poetic metaphor of "seeds" to describe sources of contemplation and of seeking God's will. He wrote, "Every moment and every event of our life on earth plants something in our soul. . . . Every expression of the will of God is in some sense a 'word' of God and therefore a 'seed' of new life" (*Seeds*, 11). Sustaining the metaphor of seeds, he added: "If I were looking for God, every event and every moment would sow, in my will, grains of God's life that would spring up one day in a tremendous harvest" (*Seeds*, 12). In his revised version, he wrote of "the possibility of an uninterrupted dialogue with God" not as continuous chatter at God but rather as "a dialogue of deep wills" (*New Seeds*, 14). He viewed the will of God as "an interior invitation of personal love" that implies "a kind of death to our exterior self" (*New Seeds*, 15). He went on to say that not everything we are and do is of God. Unfocused energy is not God's will, pressured work is not God's will (*New Seeds*, 19).

Things in their reality, their true identity, are God's will: "A tree gives glory to God by being a tree" (*Seeds*, 18). Returning to his dominant metaphor, Merton wrote: "The seeds that are planted in my liberty at every moment, by God's will, are the seeds of my own identity, my own reality, my own happiness, my own sanctity" (*Seeds*, 21). And he added: "The secret of my identity is hidden in the love and mercy of God" (*Seeds*, 23). In his revised text, he wrote that being ourselves is God's will: "Our vocation is not simply to *be*, but to work together with God in the creation of our own life, our own identity, our own destiny. . . . We are even called to share with God the work of *creating* the truth of our identity" (*New Seeds*, 32). So he urged us: "Pray for Your Own Discovery" (*Seeds*, 25–31). And is this not the thread of Merton's own life, his own struggle to find himself, his own search for his real self in God?

We see in Merton's later writings that he expanded his reflections from the individual search for God's will to the corporate, national, global search for God's will. I believe this insight enabled him to enter into meaningful dialogue with other religions. Merton returned to this theme when he wrote: " 'God's will' is certainly found in anything that is required of us in order that we may be united with one another in love" (*New Seeds*, 76).

Contemplation for Merton, then, has everything to do with seeking God's will and experiencing God's mercy. It is not removed from the reality and demands of our daily lives. Rather it opens us to the gift-dimension of our lives, a gift-dimension that can be appreciated only by faith.

In his book *Contemplative Prayer*, Merton used the desert as an image of contemplation.[34] Even though we may live in a community with others, we are bound to explore the inner waste of our own being (*Prayer*, 27). He has shifted the metaphor for contemplation here — not "seeds of contemplation," which speak of fertility and life-giving hope, but rather "the desert," which speaks of waste and inner dread. In a way, he has shifted seasons from the verdure of spring and summer to the stripping of autumn and winter. To recognize and describe these seasons of the heart is a service he renders us as spiritual guide, to acknowledge that none of us knows only the fullness of consolation or only the emptiness of desolation.

He wrote in these essays about "prayer of the heart" whereby we seek God present in the depths of our being and meet God by invoking the name of Jesus in faith, wonder, and love (*Prayer*, 30–31). This kind of prayer is rooted in the ground of our being. In this observation, Merton led us as spiritual guide beyond the intellectual or psychological analysis of our problems to the integrating acceptance of the mystery at the heart of our lives, to gratitude for the gift-dimension of our lives. In light of this, we may be heartened that prayer operates at a level deeper than our consciousness, deeper than our psyche. It is simpler than thought or feeling. It operates at the level of the heart. In the desert tradition, the heart is a source-word. It is the place where God and the demons do battle. Merton describes the heart in the following way:

It refers to the deepest psychological ground of one's personality, the inner sanctuary where self-awareness goes beyond analytical reflection and opens out into metaphysical and theological confrontation with the Abyss of the unknown yet present — one who is "more intimate to us than we are to ourselves" (to adopt the phrase from Augustine's *Confessions*). (*Prayer*, 33)

Merton showed himself to be an astute spiritual guide when he named different obstacles to prayer — presumption, spiritual inertia, confusions, coldness, lack of confidence, and discouragement. Meditation, for him, is rooted in life. What did he mean by that? Not austere penances, long hours of prayer, and separation from loved ones in and of themselves. But rather "a simple respect for the concrete realities of everyday life, for nature, for the body, for one's work, one's friends, one's surroundings, etc." (*Prayer*, 39).

Merton demonstrated his balance as spiritual guide by indicating the close connection between liturgy and contemplative prayer (*Prayer*, 46). He stood in the tradition of monastic spiritual guides with Basil, Gregory the Great, Bernard of Clairvaux, and Peter of Celles, about the relationship between prayer and work, between contemplation and action. Instead of launching into a monologue on what contemplative prayer meant to him, Merton, like any competent spiritual guide, invited the reader to review the history of this connection in the Christian monastic tradition. To be a competent spiritual guide today, it is not enough to be someone of the now generation, conversant only with the latest trend or fad in spirituality, whether that be transcendental meditation, yoga, guided imagery, Myers-Briggs, the Enneagram, or another framework. One needs a solid grounding in the history and theology of Christian spirituality in order to help people name their experience of God in the context of other people's religious experience.

Merton described the "prayer of the heart" in more detail in subsequent chapters of this book: "yearning for the simple presence of God, for a personal understanding of God's word, for knowledge of God's will, and for capacity to hear and obey God. It is thus something much more than uttering petitions for good things external to our own deepest concerns" (*Prayer*, 67). A true spiritual guide mediates interior freedom, a freedom from inordinate attachments, a freedom for the loving service of God and God's people. He argued that meditation is not a matter merely of reflecting on one's place in the universe:

We should let ourselves be brought naked and defenseless into the center of that dread where we stand alone before God in our nothingness, without explanation, without theories, completely dependent upon God's providential care, in dire need of the gift of God's grace, God's mercy and the light of faith. (*Prayer*, 69)

Merton viewed this experience of dread as crucial to a life of contemplative prayer. It is, as it were, the paschal mystery of the contemplative who lets go of needs and fears to receive gratefully the mystery of God's gift of self. The price of this letting go is self-denial and sacrifice (*Prayer*, 72).

He wrote also of a deeper dimension of the dread experienced by the contemplative, not only the desert of our unknowing but also the blindness of our brokenness, the alienation that exists between the ego and God, the basic poverty of our sinfulness. Again, Merton artfully encouraged us to view this experience of dread not as punishing but as purifying. He saw the positive way that dread can help us relativize the seriousness with which we view our progress in the spiritual life: "Dread is an expression of our insecurity in this earthly life, a realization that we are never and can never be completely 'sure' in the sense of *possessing* a definitive and established spiritual status."[35] He regarded this experience of poverty as a vital dimension of our Christ-consciousness, as an essential aspect of our living the paschal mystery existentially, as an essential prerequisite to celebrating the paschal mystery liturgically (*Prayer*, 106). This poverty is our powerlessness.

For Merton, creative intuition was analogous to contemplative intuition.[36] His poetic vision of reality gave a depth to his contemplative vision and evoked that depth in other poets.[37] His contemplative vision expressed itself in photography and in his attraction to sacred art.[38] And throughout his life, Merton struggled with his vocation to be an artist and a monk.[39]

Our union with God depends for Merton on a twofold movement whereby we enter into ourselves and transcend ourselves. In so doing, we shift from living out of our isolated ego to living out of our liberated true self that is dependent on others and God in the Spirit.[40]

For him, contemplation meant seeking God's will and finding God's mercy. It was his way to mutual interdependence with other people, nature, and the world.

Conclusion

Thomas Merton as a spiritual guide speaks to us of a personal integrity that kept him faithful to his own search for God. His life portrays the necessity of solitude in nurturing interiority and enabling us to live at *le point vierge* of our being. He illumines the healing power of accepting ourselves as we are and an integration that includes accepting brokenness, our own and that of others. For him, spiritual guidance is not directing another to follow fixed norms, but freeing the other to follow the Holy Spirit. He speaks of the value of peace in making prayerful decisions and choices in faith. And he shows contemplation as a way of life that seeks God's will in all and experiences God's tender mercies daily.

Merton is a spiritual guide for today. As a religious, he did much for ecumenism and interfaith dialogue. He took the time and trouble to read and reflect on books by contemporary Protestant theologians like Karl Barth and Dietrich Bonhoeffer. He corresponded with Protestants, Orthodox Christians, Jews, Hindus, Buddhists, Zen Buddhists, and Muslims. He studied Sufism and Taoism. He shows us how to broaden our perspectives and enter into views and values other than our own. His openness to change and his willingness to allow his thought to develop continually can inspire us to greater flexibility while remaining rooted in our faith.

Merton's life experience was his own spiritual guide. He joins those whose autobiography is spirituality, whose life story itself reveals God's presence and mystery. The very fact that Merton kept and published so many journals is testimony to his recognition of the value of telling his story as a help in discerning the pattern of God's unique and personal action in his own life, and later on, in the life of the church and of the world.

After Vatican II, Merton continued to let life experience be his own spiritual guide. And now his concerns were not only personal, but also local, national, ecclesial, ecumenical, and global in scope.

Many who helped to form his mind and heart were in turn formed by him. Some whom he had helped to form ended up having an impact on his growth and development. In this regard, Merton is prophetic of a mutuality that is characteristic of spiritual direction today.

Perhaps we will come to find that Merton's greatest contribution to the church and to the world was not his writing but his life, a life marked always by the cross lived first in his dysfunctional family and then in the austerity of a religious order, a life given to creative self-expression but also to redemptive self-emptying.[41] By fidelity to his call to contemplation, he came to realize the socio-political implications of the commandment to love our neighbor.[42]

Merton challenges us to rethink North American Christianity for the twenty-first century. His solitary life engaged him in a compassionate concern for the world. His self-acceptance opened him to communicate with a variety of writers and thinkers, many of whom were non-Catholic and non-Christian. His spiritual guidance has a ring of authenticity about it, since his wisdom was his life. His struggle for peace led to his position of nonviolent resistance to militarism and racism. His contemplative vision drew him to commit himself anew to the world he had renounced by becoming a monk.

Merton wrote about the heart as the psychological ground of our personality. Karl Rahner goes one step further, by calling the heart the center of our freedom, the place where we surrender to the mystery of God, the place where Jesus surrendered to the mystery of God.[43] Merton comes close to Rahner's description of the heart when he writes: "My true identity lies hidden in God's call to my freedom and my response to God. This means I must use my freedom in order to *love*, with full responsibility and authenticity" (*Prayer*, 68).

Merton urged respect for the concrete realities of daily life, like Karl Rahner's mysticism of everyday faith, of daily love that seeks to contemplate God's love and presence in the simplest aspects and encounters of our lives: taking a walk, sipping a cup of coffee, or listening to music.[44]

His contribution to North American spirituality is immense. He integrated in himself the call to prayer and the call to social action. His vehicle to deplore the ills of society was writing. He enabled many to be free to experience contemplative prayer. At the same time, he insisted that being a Christian in the world today meant living in and for the world, taking a stand, for example, on the cold war, on racism, and on the Vietnam war.

His contribution to Catholicism in North America is significant. A convert, he absorbed the classics of tradition. A monk, he embodied the values of Vatican II and strove to challenge the church to take its place in the modern world, not as a triumphalistic bastion of certitude and security, but as a humble seeker of the truth open to dialogue and seeking to do justice in faith. He integrated the secular in a contemplative way, gradually becoming convinced of the church's need to be open to the world, its beauty and its anguish.

His contribution to monasticism is incalculable. He was a leader in monastic renewal. He made Western Catholic monasticism accessible to many Christians by his writings and opened the door for Christian and non-Christian nuns and monks to communicate with one another in the United States and throughout the world. He had a particular interest in the renewal of Christian monasticism in Asia. While he wished always to live and pray simply in solitude and silence, he could not deny his call and compulsion to write. He chose to become and remain a Cistercian monk, paving the way for other monks in his own order to live as hermits.[45]

His contribution to the peace movement in North America is beyond measure. He stated positions at a time when it was unfashionable and dangerous to do so. His writings on war and peace may have been most effective not as ethical guidelines for Roman Catholics but as moral support to leaders active in the peace movement. His writings on racial justice were another form of his commitment to nonviolent resistance and proved to be accurate predictions of the course of events that took place in the 1960s in the United States. His spiritual leadership took concrete shape when he led the leaders of the future Catholic Pacifist movement in a retreat at his hermitage. Had he lived he would surely have reflected upon and incorporated the key insights of liberation theology.[46]

Merton was comfortable praying in silence or in words, writing in prose or poetry. He holds out to us the value of silence and the value of dialogue, the value of the nonverbal and the value of words. He journeyed to the East at the end of his life not just as a lecturer and a research scholar, but above all as a pilgrim wanting to live his own life more deeply.[47]

Merton the monk-writer invites us to know and tell our own story, the story of our journey to God. He knew himself to be a monk (*monachos*), one called to solitude. He knew himself to be a mystery, a secret known only to God. He lived this mystery in the secret of solitude. He gave us glimpses of this mystery in his prose and poetry, but always he pointed us not to himself but to our own real self and to God. Elena Malits comments: "Merton has taught us to appreciate the theological significance of the quest for self-identity."[48] His spirituality is mystical, political, pluralist, secular, ecumenical, socially conscientized, transcultural, and global.

While he valued the contemplative life, he realized the idol he could make of it. He learned to value contemplative life as a life lived with depth and integrity from a contemplative dimension. Aware that he could close himself off to the world, he welcomed the opportunity to enter into the hopes and the fears of humankind. This he did by speaking out against war and violence, by praying for peace, by listening to other people, and by making his own experience available to those who were interested. He can teach us how to embrace the world with compassion.

Merton learned to integrate his spiritual and intellectual growth and development with his emotional adolescence. He had learned early on that our knowledge of our true self is our knowledge of God. In his writing, he returned again and again to this theme. It is paradoxical that even though the search for self-identity was his constant theme, it is difficult to describe him in a few words. He is not considered a systematic theologian; he did not consider himself a prophet.[49] I am not drawn to his poetry but have been helped immensely by his journals. He was a mystic who contemplated God in the world and a religious mentor whose life of solitude and community, of silence and conversation with the world is and perhaps remains the acid test of his message. I am not convinced that he was intent on communicating a message; I am convinced that he was interested above all in living a mystery, the mystery of who he was before God, a living mystery of solitude.

READINGS

Outstanding in Thomas Merton's autobiographical writing are *The Seven Storey Mountain* (New York: Harcourt Brace Jovanovich, 1976) and *The Sign of Jonas* (Garden City, N.Y.: Doubleday, Image, 1960). *New Seeds of Contemplation* (New York: New Directions, 1961) reflects his growing understanding of contemplation as providing one with a theology for life. The shift in his thinking in the late 1950s and early 1960s is signaled by his *Conjectures of a Guilty Bystander* (Garden City, N.Y.: Doubleday, Image, 1968) and *Disputed Questions* (New York: Farrar, Straus & Cudahy, 1960). *The Asian Journal of Thomas Merton*, ed. Naomi Burton et al. (New York: New Directions, 1975) records his journey to the East.

Three fine collections of his letters have been published: *The Hidden Ground of Love: The Letters of Thomas Merton on Religious Experience and Social Concerns*, ed. William H. Shannon (New York: Farrar, Straus & Giroux, 1985); *The Road to Joy: The Letters of Thomas Merton to New and Old Friends*, ed. Robert E. Daggy (New York: Farrar, Straus & Giroux, 1989); and *The School of Charity: The Letters of Thomas*

Merton on Religious Renewal and Spiritual Direction, ed. Patrick Hart, O.C.S.O. (New York: Farrar, Straus & Giroux, 1990).

Several recent works by Merton have appeared: *A Vow of Conversation: Journals 1964–1965*, ed. Naomi Burton Stone (New York: Farrar, Straus & Giroux, 1988); *Thomas Merton: Preview of the Asian Journey*, ed. Walter H. Capps (New York: Crossroad, 1989); and Thomas Merton, *Thomas Merton in Alaska. Prelude to The Asian Journal: The Alaskan Conferences, Journals and Letters* (New York: New Directions, 1989).

Monica Furlong wrote *Merton: A Biography* (San Francisco: Harper & Row, 1980), and Elena Malits wrote *The Solitary Explorer: Thomas Merton's Transforming Journey* (San Francisco: Harper & Row, 1980). Michael Mott wrote the authoritative biography, *The Seven Mountains of Thomas Merton* (Boston: Houghton Mifflin, 1984).

To trace the shift in Merton's thinking about social concerns, consult James Baker's important work, *Thomas Merton, Social Critic* (Lexington, Ky.: University Press of Kentucky, 1971). To understand the tension under which he lived as both a writer and a monk, read Victor A. Kramer's helpful study, *Thomas Merton* (Boston: Twayne, 1984), and David D. Cooper's penetrating study, *Thomas Merton's Art of Denial: The Evolution of a Radical Humanist* (Athens, Ga.: University of Georgia Press, 1989).

On his theology of mysticism, see Raymond Bailey, *Thomas Merton on Mysticism* (Garden City, N.Y.: Doubleday, Image, 1976); and William H. Shannon, *Thomas Merton's Dark Path: The Inner Experience of a Contemplative* (New York: Farrar, Straus & Giroux, 1981). On his theology of prayer, see John J. Higgins, S.J., *Thomas Merton on Prayer* (Garden City, N.Y.: Doubleday & Co., 1973). On his theology of the self, see Anne E. Carr's significant synthesis, *A Search for Wisdom and Spirit: Thomas Merton's Theology of the Self* (Notre Dame: University of Notre Dame Press, 1988). On his theology of social responsibility, see Frederic J. Kelly, S.J., *Man before God: Thomas Merton on Social Responsibility* (Garden City, N.Y.: Doubleday, 1974).

6

HENRI NOUWEN

(1932–)

Prophet of Conversion

HENRI NOUWEN is a prophet of conversion. He is a Dutch priest, clinical psychologist, pastoral theologian, and spiritual writer living at l'Arche Daybreak, a Christian community in Toronto. His writings, his lectures, and his lifestyle speak to us of a man in search of his true self, a man reaching out to others, a man in search of God.

Born in Holland in 1932, the oldest of three brothers and one sister, Nouwen as a child lived through World War II. He entered the diocesan seminary at age eighteen and was ordained. After studying at the University of Nijmegen from 1957 to 1964, he engaged in clinical-pastoral education at the Menninger Clinic in Topeka, Kansas, until 1966. He taught at the University of Notre Dame, and then in Holland. After further theology studies, he taught pastoral theology at both Yale University Divinity School and Harvard Divinity School. During his time at Yale, he spent two sabbaticals in prolonged prayer at the Trappist Abbey of the Genesee. After Yale, he spent six months in Bolivia and Peru to discern whether he was being called to work with the poor in Latin America. At present, he lives at l'Arche Daybreak in Toronto, serving as chaplain and continuing to write and lecture.

Nouwen is a prophet of conversion, more specifically in the sense of a "second" or affective conversion. Conversion means a turning to God, a being turned to God. After an initial conversion experience, people in the Western Christian tradition often prepare to be baptized, ordained, consecrated to religious life, or committed in a significant way to solidarity with poor and oppressed people. Our conversion, however, is never once and for all. The grace of conversion is being in love with God; it can penetrate many levels of our being: intellectual, moral, religious, and psychic.[1] Grace itself can be experienced as the lifelong process of conversion.[2]

Within this process, one can detect a "second" or affective conversion that penetrates our disordered affections, our unintegrated feelings, our range of moods and emotions.[3] It reaches down beneath our practices of piety and acts of religion to the very wellsprings of our faith and doubt, our hope and despair, our capacity to love and our selfishness. It is not an invitation to change, to behave differently, to act always out of our best self. Rather, it is a call to accept ourselves, others, and God. It is above all the grace to accept God's acceptance of us, to receive God's intimacy, to know that we are loved deeply and held closely.[4]

His own message springs from a self-knowledge based on an acknowledgement of his brokenness and a celebration of his giftedness. He is willing to seek God in faith and to struggle with his self-doubts and fears of rejection. Even in discouragement and disappointment, he chooses to trust in God's providence. He reaches out to love others, painfully conscious of his own needs for affection and reconciliation. Over and over again, Nouwen turned from his problems to the mystery of God's loving us, and from professionalism to his personal relationship with God, the real source of his self-esteem. Over and over again, he turned from Pelagian efforts to please others to a freeing receptivity to God's forgiving nearness. Nouwen is not alone. He holds out to us the possibility of ongoing affective conversion by making accessible the reality of his own life-experience. He mediates to us an acceptance of ourselves, others, and God, by telling us about his own growth in this attitude of heart.

This conversion process that moves through self-acceptance leads him to a strong sense of mission. He is convinced that we are called to a change that is as radical as revolution and is not separate from revolution. He sees the connections between changing the human heart and changing human society. Moreover we are not converted in order to remain individualistic, but to help build community. Our commitment to love our neighbor has socio-political implications.

Are we open to the surprise of God's love or are we intent on planning and controlling events? Are we afraid to be alone or do we welcome solitude as a place of revelation? Is ministry a job for which we are paid, a career in which we are advancing, or our simple service to others in the name of Jesus? Do we look for self-esteem from the approval of others or in our relationship with God? Do we wait for God to reveal our mission in the world or are we convinced we know our purpose in life?

In this chapter, I describe how five insights into conversion are grounded in Nouwen's life-experience: openness to conversion, solitude as the place of conversion, ministry as fostering conversion, a sense of identity and a sense of mission as fruits of conversion. I discuss these insights in Nouwen's works. Finally, I reflect on Nouwen's pedagogy as inviting conversion. By leading us to conversion, he serves as a valuable spiritual guide for today.[5]

His Own Conversion Process: A Paradigm

Henri Nouwen writes often about the process of conversion, reflecting at the same time on his own conversion. His life, in fact, is a paradigm illustrating the insights he articulates.

Openness to Conversion

His openness to conversion is evident in his efforts to place himself in situations that could turn his heart to God. He came initially to the United States in order to add a pastoral dimension to his studies in theology and psychology. He spent time in Peru and Bolivia exploring the possibility of a call to live in the Third World. He has had prolonged stays at the Trappist Abbey of the Genesee for spiritual renewal. His involvement with l'Arche in Trosly-Breuil and in Toronto is a concrete way of living solidarity with poor people in a community of shared faith. "These moves indicate a continuing search, an evolving spirituality reaching out to others, the life of a pilgrim and prophet."[6]

The Road to Daybreak reveals Nouwen's enduring openness to conversion, his struggle to follow Jesus more radically, his willingness to leave a successful academic career in order to continue a spiritual journey by living and writing at l'Arche, a faith community of handicapped people.[7] His openness to conversion is not so much an openness to change himself as an openness to accept himself just the way he is with his need for affection and forgiveness, his restlessness and loneliness, his individualism and competitiveness.[8]

He struggles with his need to pray, his longing to follow Jesus, and his desire to stay close to Jesus, to be rooted in God. He appreciates the counter-cultural values of l'Arche: care, not competence; the sharing of gifts, not equal rights; and a fellowship of the weak, not of efficiency and power. His openness to conversion offers us spiritual guidance by affirming our need for self-acceptance and emphasizing the prophetic dynamism of gospel values.[9]

Solitude as the Place of Conversion

If Nouwen has experienced solitude as the place of his own conversion, it is because he has valued the "desert" of going apart to pray. He has carved out of his busy schedule times for prolonged prayer daily and periodically for months at a stretch. His times of prayer at the Genesee Abbey are a striking example of the fruit he draws from solitude. *A Cry for Mercy* records prayers that he wrote during his six-month stay from February to August 1979. In the epilogue, he affirms in hindsight how this solitude had become a place of conversion: "These prayers are only the context for prayer. If anything has become clear, it is that I cannot pray, but that the Spirit of God prays in me"(*Cry*, 173). Another way in which Nouwen experiences solitude as the place of his own conversion is his being drawn to pray contemplatively.[10]

Ministry as Fostering Conversion

Nouwen taught courses on ministry and spirituality during his years at Yale Divinity School from 1971 to 1981, and then at Harvard Divinity School from 1983 to 1985. He was aware that theological education for ministry does not always foster conversion. It can reinforce competition and become an idolatry of the mind. Nouwen's own experience of studying and teaching theology are reflected in his first book, *Intimacy*, in which he describes his attempt from 1966 to 1968 to help priests and priest candidates at Notre Dame to integrate their academic pursuits with their pastoral concerns.

A Sense of Identity as a Fruit of Conversion

In *Beyond the Mirror,* Nouwen reflects on his deepened sense of identity as a fruit of a conversion. In an accident that could have been fatal, he was hit by the rearview mirror of a van, fell, broke five ribs, and nearly bled to death. The removal of his spleen meant the gift of life renewed. Before the surgery, he took the time to prepare for death and discovered that the hardest separation he could imagine was not from loved ones but from those he had not yet forgiven or who had not forgiven him. Within this deep desire to forgive and be forgiven, Nouwen experienced God's pure and unconditional love (*Mirror*, 15–48). This accident became for him an opportunity of conversion.

One of the fruits of conversion is a sense of personal identity in God. During his recuperation, Nouwen rediscovered the heart of his vocation: to live with a growing desire to be with God and to proclaim this love to others. *Beyond the Mirror* was a direct result of this new sense of vocation. He was to speak about the presence of God always and everywhere, to witness to the ways of God acting in the world. Exploring the implications of his new sense of identity led him to question his values: power or service, visibility or hiddenness, success or faithfulness to his vocation. He saw more clearly that his sense of belonging to God could free him to feel with others. He realized in a more radical way that he was called to contemplative prayer, silence, solitude, and detachment. From this perspective, he views his accident as a reminder of his identity, as a call from God (*Mirror*, 9).[11]

In *Canvas of Love*, Nouwen records his mirror experiences in the context of Rembrandt's painting of "The Return of the Prodigal Son" (*Love*). His profound contemplation of this painting enables him to have a mirror experience with each of its three main characters, that is, to identify with the prodigal son, the elder brother, and the compassionate father. This exercise deepens his sense of his own identity in God as a fruit of conversion.

He calls his encounter with this painting a homecoming and uses the metaphor of returning and leaving home in every chapter of this book. Through this parable, Nouwen discovers a new aspect of his vocation, that of speaking and writing from the place of the home of God within himself about the restlessness in his own life and the lives of others. For him, this gospel story of the prodigal son is a question of vocation (*Love*, Prologue).

Nouwen has no difficulty identifying with the younger son who squandered his wealth and returned to his father, owning once again his identity of sonship with its rights and responsibilities. The author sees in himself the mentality of the younger son, wanting to take what was his and separate himself from parental lineage. Nouwen experiences that we are and remain children of God throughout our lives, always needing the safety of home and of God's forgiveness (*Love*, part 1).

As he continues to meditate on this painting, Nouwen begins to see himself in the elder son as well. He identifies with the elder brother being lost while still at home, letting resentment rob him of joy, trying to redeem himself, being invited to trust and gratitude (*Love*, part 2).

In time, Nouwen could also claim the father's role as an intrinsic part of his identity, allowing himself not only to feel the maternal care and paternal support of the hands of God, but also to extend his own hands in blessing. This painting reminds Nouwen that the spiritual life is not so much a self-conscious effort to find God but rather a surrender to God's unconditional love. It helps him see that the real struggle is to accept himself and to accept God's "first love" of him. One detail that Nouwen dwells on is that the father in Luke's gospel account calls for a celebration as a paradigm of how our healing God invites us to live a joyful life. This mystery of reconciliation needs to be nourished by a community where we feel at home, stay at home, and make home for others (*Love*, part 3 and Epilogue).

Different events can promote our ongoing conversion. In Nouwen's case, his accident and his prolonged contemplation of Rembrandt's painting were two events that have shed light on his identity in God. His willingness to pray over both experiences invites us to find God in our daily lives.

His growing appreciation for the communal dimension of conversion has been influenced, no doubt, by his experiences of community life at the Trappist Abbey of the Genesee and at l'Arche. His journals written at Genesee speak of the ways he shared faith in silence with the monks, praying the Office and eating meals, as well as in his conversations with Abbot John Eudes Bamberger. In his years of teaching at Yale and Harvard, he increasingly felt the need for a supportive community of faith as a context for his ministry. His book *The Road to Daybreak* recounts his call to share life and faith with the l'Arche community of handicapped people, first in Trosly and now in Toronto.

A Sense of Mission as a Fruit of Conversion

Very much a man of his times, Nouwen perceives the global implications of conversion, that is, the socio-political and socio-critical aspects of love of our neighbor. He does not restrict himself to First World countries. A few years ago, he chose in faith to live in solidarity with poor people in Third World countries to discern his own mission. And in these situations, he tried not only to live with the poor, but also to learn about their plight. He attended Gustavo Gutiérrez's summer course on a spirituality of liberation in Lima, Peru, and talked with Miguel D'Escoto in Nicaragua. His searching becomes a shared experience in the awakening of our conscience and raising of our social consciousness.

Nouwen's search to live in solidarity with the poor is also closely connected to his call to peacemaking. His sense of mission impels him to see peace as a gift received in prayer, to resist all the forces of death, and to affirm the signs of life joyfully.[12] His identification with suffering people as a form of identification with Jesus is a fruit of his conversion. By recounting his experiences in Latin America, Nouwen inspires us to look beyond our borders to enter into solidarity with the oppressed.

In summary, his own conversion process is a paradigm of the insights he explores. He himself is open to his own conversion. He values solitude as a place of encounter with God. In ministry he not only gives but is transformed by those he serves. He brings to the task of theology the call to pray and proclaim the Word of God. Through events, he learns that he is deeply loved by God and sent to discover and reveal this love to others.

Five Insights into Conversion

Having viewed his life as a paradigm of the conversion process, one can trace the same themes in his writings.

Openness to Conversion

One theme that characterizes Nouwen's spiritual guidance in his writings is openness to the process of conversion. In Nouwen's book *With Open Hands*, his image of conversion is the image of open hands, not clinging, not clenched, but rather open to receive and to share, open to let others come in and to let go. Opening our hands before God means accepting existence readily "not as a possession to defend, but as a gift to receive."[13]

Nouwen writes in *The Wounded Healer* about how our own experience of the wound of loneliness can be a source of healing to others, if we accept this very painful wound in our own lives, not denying it or neglecting it (*Healer*, 87). This does not mean talking about our personal struggles with loneliness, but creating a space within ourselves where we can welcome the other as guest in the home of our heart. Such hospitality implies a self-emptying and a centeredness, as Nouwen perceives: "Then our presence is no longer threatening and demanding but inviting and liberating" (*Healer*, 92). Here hospitality is viewed as an openness to others springing from an openness to ourselves.

Similarly, in *Aging*, Nouwen and Walter Gaffney, his co-author, underline two principles of pastoral care for the elderly: "We are called to make our own aging self the main instrument of our healing.... Caring for the aging is not a special type of care."[14] The authors invite our openness to conversion by insisting that real care happens when we find each other on the common ground of the human condition, when we recognize and accept our own process of growing old, and when we treat the elderly with the same respect and appreciation with which we treat ourselves and others.

In *The Genesee Diary*, Nouwen reflects on Abbot John Eudes Bamberger's insight that bridges the psychological and the spiritual dimensions of growth: "In meditation we can come to the affirmation that we are not created by other people but by God, that we are not judged by how we compare with others but how we fulfill the will of God" (*Genesee*, 74). Thus openness to conversion represents a shift from basing our self-esteem on others' approval to discovering our self-worth based on God's acceptance, a shift away from competition that gives too much authority to others, to obedience that trusts our own inner authority.

Solitude as the Place of Conversion

A second way in which Nouwen guides us is to experience and reflect on solitude as the place of conversion. In *Thomas Merton: Contemplative Critic*, he observes how Merton discovered solitude as the place of his conversion for growth not only in self-knowledge, but also in empathy with others in their brokenness. The concluding paradox provides the following insight: "Precisely because Merton had discovered this non-violent compassion in his solitude could he in a real sense be a monk, that is to say, one who unmasks through his criticism the illusions of a violent society and who wants to change the world in spirit and truth" (*Merton*, 38–66). In *Clowning in Rome*, Nouwen's talks to priests studying in Rome, he says that solitude "sets us free from the compulsions of fear and anger," and adds that it "diverts us from our fears and anger and makes us empty for God" (*Rome*, 14, 31). Part of our relationship with God is not trying to get rid of or get beyond our fear and anger, but sharing with God our fears and angers, allowing God to heal us by helping us accept them and let go of them.

Fundamentally, solitude is the way of the heart. In his book *The Way of the Heart*, Nouwen describes those compulsive ministers who are afraid of solitude and constantly look for affirmation outside themselves (*Way*, 10). Speaking of the fourth century desert writers, Nouwen observes: "For them solitude is not a private therapeutic place. Rather, it is the place of conversion" (*Way*, 15). Solitude then is not an end in itself; it is the place where we can be transformed into loving people:

"Charity, not silence, is the purpose of the spiritual life and of ministry" (*Way*, 47).

His valuing of solitude as the place of conversion offers us spiritual guidance to re-discover the way of the heart. This way is simple yet demanding, centering yet also humbling.

Ministry as Fostering Conversion

A third way in which Henri Nouwen can be a spiritual guide for us is in his attitude toward ministry as a way to foster conversion, not simply to increase knowledge. For him ministry is faith seeking healing both for those to whom one is ministering and for oneself.

In a pamphlet called *From Resentment to Gratitude*, Nouwen challenges seminarians to let go of their resentment and be healed by gratitude for effective ministry. As wounded healers, they can serve others with the empathy learned through their own experiences of suffering. From this perspective, he views seminary education as education to the Eucharist and to a eucharistic life based on unending gratitude.[15]

While the image of "wounded healer" touches on the paradox of how we give life out of death, the image of "living reminder" points to the sacramentality of our service to others. Nouwen describes the minister as a living reminder of Christ, a reminder that is healing, sustaining, and guiding. As living reminders, we are invited to withdraw periodically from those we serve in order to be in the presence of God.[16]

In *Creative Ministry*, he reminds us that "individual pastoral care can never be limited to the application of any skill or technique since ultimately it is the continuing search for God in the life of the people we want to serve" (*Ministry*, 63). He shows that the movement from professionalism in ministry to a spirituality of ministry is a conversion: a movement that includes both self-affirmation and self-sacrifice, a movement from a legalistic notion of contract to the biblical notion of covenant, a movement from role-definition to careful and critical contemplation (*Ministry*, 41–65).

In "The Monk and the Cripple," Nouwen describes the powerlessness of ministers who, living in the name of Jesus, see God in unexpected places. What ministers offer to others is solidarity in powerlessness. This means resisting the temptation to dominate and voluntarily choosing powerlessness that knows its need to live with others in community and to make visible a shared faith and love. Shared weakness reveals shared strength. Implicit in the call to healthy and mature ministry is the mandate to serve other ministers in a mutuality of ministry. This approach to ministry is possible only if contemplative prayer is seen as the basis and center of ministry. Spending time with Jesus strengthens us to know the ministerial value of prayer. It helps us see that those we serve reveal to us by their suffering the compassionate heart of Jesus. It also enables us to see God's presence in our lives in such a way that we become capable of revealing God's presence to others, helping them discover God's face in their lives. Our pastoral care of others prepares them to celebrate God's healing power in a communal way.[17]

Thus our ministry fosters our conversion process, freeing us to let go of our need to be in control. It helps us to feel comfortable with powerlessness, our own and that of others. It turns us again and again to Christ for strength, healing, and guidance, whereby Christ becomes the center of our lives. It heals us to see God at work in the simplest details and demands and delights of daily life. Knowing we are wounded healers, we are free to mediate God's healing to others, not by bandaging their wounds but by helping them heal themselves.

For Nouwen, it is not only ministry that fosters conversion but also theological education in preparation for ministry. He urges religion teachers to affirm people's search for God by allowing painful questions to be raised. Teaching religion thus strengthens the human quest for meaning. By their willingness to be wounded healers, religion teachers can invite others to reflect on their call to conversion in their lived experiences of painful growth.[18]

In "Theology as Doxology: Reflections on Theological Education," he emphasizes prayer, community, and ministry as formative in theological education. Without prayer viewed as the praise of God, our theology can remain a competitive academic discipline finely honed in critical analysis, but alienated from contemplative awareness. Without community, the place of common vulnerability, our theology can reinforce isolating individualism and intellectual argument without nurturing a life of faith. Without ministry, in the sense of proclamation of the Word of God, our theology can disclaim the Word of God by keeping the knowledge of God to itself instead of sharing it with others.[19]

We can take to heart Nouwen's reflections on "Studying Theology as Doxology." When he writes of "Listening to the Word," he urges us to listen to our own hearts, to each other, and to God speaking to us through our reading and life experience. We call each other to have a listening heart. His section on "Speaking the Word" encourages not debate and argument but an atmosphere of faith sharing and theological reflection. His section on "Reading the Word" inspires theology students to read the book of their lives while reading their assignments. Homework can become spiritual reading because of the contemplative and reflective manner in which it is approached. In these ways, theology students can form among themselves not only an academic community of those seeking the truth and completing course requirements, but also a community of shared faith, helping one another to get in touch with the truth of their being. In his section on "Writing the Word," he makes this comment: "In theological education it is of great importance to rediscover writing as a spiritual discipline by which we can come to discern the active presence of God among us."[20]

Nouwen believes that ministry as well as theological education for ministry can foster conversion. He shows us how to become wounded healers and living reminders for others. It is clear that for Nouwen theological education goes hand in hand with discerning God's presence in one's personal prayer, in community where faith is shared, and in ministry where God's word is proclaimed.

A Sense of Identity as a Fruit of Conversion

A fourth point of emphasis in Nouwen's works is a deepened sense of identity as a fruit of conversion. This sense of identity is nourished not only by solitude but by a community of shared faith. We do not turn to God alone.

In his book called *Reaching Out*, he reflects on the communal dimension of prayer, that is to say, the communal dimension of conversion. Prayer is to be shared with others because it arises from the heart of our lives, and at the same time, it needs the support and protection of a community of faith for its growth (*Reaching*, 139).

Members of a community of faith can grow by sharing with each other the fruits of contemplation, their life with God, and their times of solitude: "Being alone with God for yourself," he says in his book *Clowning in Rome*, "is a very different experience from being alone with God as part of your life together" (*Rome*, 23).

In *Making All Things New*, Nouwen writes about a sense of identity in God as a fruit of conversion. Our spiritual life is real only when it is lived in our daily joys and pains. What can block us from conversion is being busy or being preoccupied with many things. What can call us to conversion is the one necessary thing: "Jesus does not speak about a change of activities, a change in contacts, or even a change of pace. He speaks about a change of heart. This change of heart makes everything different, even while everything appears to remain the same" (*New*, 42).[21] This change of heart is required for living a spiritual life. Although it can happen through a sudden change or a slow process of transformation, it is always experienced as a sense of oneness. Solitude and community are two disciplines of prayer that strengthen and solidify this change of heart (*New*, 57, 65–95). Three other disciplines of the spiritual life are the discipline of the church whereby we let the paschal mystery form and inform us, the discipline of scriptural meditation in order to recognize God's word speaking directly to our hearts, and the discipline of spiritual direction in order to discern God's presence in our lives.[22]

In "A Sudden Trip to Lourdes," Nouwen reflects on aspects of his sense of identity that were renewed on a three-day trip to Lourdes in January of 1990. At the grotto of Our Lady of Lourdes, he experienced a call to purity, simplicity, and innocence that simplified his desires and reminded him that in this new decade he wants to let Jesus become the center of his life, the heart of his heart, the lover of his soul, and the bridegroom of his spirit. Notice that he views himself not according to the things he does but from within his personal relationship with Christ. For him, this is his call to conversion, to keep his gaze fixed on Jesus and to let Jesus have a significant influence on more and more of his daily life. His sense of worth is based, then, not on his achievements nor on his affective relationships, but on his personal relationship with Christ mediated by Mary.[23]

In "Our True Spiritual Identity," Nouwen speaks of our sense of identity based on the words of consecration at the celebration of the Eucharist: we are taken, broken, blessed, and given. It is hard for us to believe that we are called as God's chosen people. This tendency to reject ourselves keeps us needing affirmation from outside. This is fostered by a discipline of the mind to realize we are first chosen, and second we are blessed since God says to each of us, "You are my beloved. On you my favor rests." We need to stop compensating for not being good enough and grow still enough to hear that reassuring voice within. We need the discipline of the heart that is prayer, a way of staying home. If we believe in God's deep acceptance of us, we do not expect a return and we can handle rejection without always seeking approval. In this conversion, we can love our brokenness, not as an interruption but as an opportunity to give ourselves; in this we are blessed. This attitude demands the discipline of the human spirit whereby we are free to hand over our burden to God in trust. Lastly, we are called to be given as Jesus gave himself, not holding private thoughts and feelings back. This attitude requires the discipline of the body whereby we try to integrate whatever happens at an emotional, sexual, affective, and intellectual level with our prayer.[24]

Conversion gives us a sense of our identity in God. This sense of identity can be experienced when we are alone and when we share faith with others.

A Sense of Mission as a Fruit of Conversion

A fifth aspect of Nouwen's spiritual guidance is his keen awareness of a renewed sense of mission as a fruit of conversion. He shows the global implications of conversion. In *Compassion*, Nouwen writes with Donald McNeill and Douglas Morrison that voluntary displacement is a form of discipleship whereby we respond to a call from the ordinary and proper place "to the places where people hurt and where we can experience with them our common human brokenness and our common need for healing."[25]

Nouwen takes into account the socio-political context of suffering in our world in his more recent books. In *Gracias!*, for example, he develops his notion of the fellowship of the weak who are happy in God because they have nothing to hide or to lose: they share their brokenness humbly and openly with one another and receive life as gift.[26] He claims that Latin America can give North America its gift of gratitude, of celebrating and sharing life.

His admiration for others' sense of mission reveals the global implications of conversion. In *Love in a Fearful Land*, he tells the stories of Stanley Rother and John Vesey, two North American missionary priests in Guatemala.[27] Nouwen shows how their call to conversion led them to a voluntary displacement on another continent that cost Rother his life.

In *Lifesigns*, he shows the connection between truth and solidarity: "We truthfully belong together in God. This is the spiritual basis for solidarity."[28] This insight shows us a global dimension of intimacy with God.

Nouwen's renewed sense of mission gives us the image of walking with Jesus as we walk with the poor, seeing Jesus suffering when we enter into their pain and fragility. In *Walk with Jesus*, Nouwen meditates on paintings of many people from different countries in various walks of life who carry the cross of Jesus in their lives: a little Vietnamese boy left behind, a Nicaraguan woman who lost her son in the war, a Sudanese man dying, a young Salvadorean woman mourning the death of her husband. His reflections invite us to walk with Jesus on this contemporary way of the cross and open our hearts to the global concerns of Christ's heart. He asks what it means to walk with the poor and sees that it means recognizing our own poverty so that we can enter into solidarity with others who are poor, and precious because they are loved by God (*Walk*, 3–98).

The conversion process is key in the spiritual journey. It touches every fiber of our being. Nouwen's insights into this process as something that goes beyond our narrow isolated situation offer us spiritual guidance in our attitude of openness, our need for solitude, our understanding of ministry and theological education as fostering ministry, our sense of identity in God, and our sense of mission.

His Pedagogy as an Invitation to Conversion

Henri Nouwen's starting point is always his personal experience of the God of his heart.[29] He follows the way of his heart. He uses different media like personal journals, preached sermons, public lectures, class notes, student seminars, books, and tapes to communicate the same message: every feeling and experience is redeemable, that is, capable of opening us to God's healing presence in Christ. Thus he considers autobiography and biography as spirituality.[30]

Nouwen writes as he relates, that is, with immediacy and authenticity. One has the feeling that he has nothing to hide and nothing to lose. His own depth and sensitivity evoke our depth and sensitivity. His creative integration of readings from different fields produces fresh images that convey some of his main points. In comparison with some contemporary spiritual writers, he shows "a greater feel for the actual modern condition and a deeper understanding of contemporary psychology."[31]

His style is not to string together undigested quotable quotes, but to put his life experience integrated in faith in dialogue with the reflections of others: poets, prophets, other spiritual guides, you and me. To get a point across, he often contrasts it with its opposite, for example, deafness and listening, refusal and obedience.

Nouwen's view of others is relational. Even his book titles and chapters underline this basic stance. *Reaching Out*, for example, explores our relationship with ourselves, others, and God in a way that excludes hierarchical thinking. His constant stress on hospitality and creating community is counter-cultural to the clock-time rigidity and individualism that color our lives. He challenges us to accept inclusive ways of living.

Nouwen's pedagogy is a pedagogy of conversion that illustrates how ministry can foster conversion. He uses "a spiritual pedagogy" whereby he creates a space for obedience to the truth and points to the principles and issues underlying questions people ask him.[32] His method of educating is experiential and pastoral. He takes the risk of sharing himself in intimacy, of reaching out of his solitude in compassion to offer us the fruits of his integration of life and prayer. He does not offer a manual of techniques nor a list of sources. Now and then he will include an excerpt from his journal or from a book he has been reading. But above all, he stays with his own experience of living in the presence of God, of integrating his life experience with his faith. He does not advise or insist. He merely invites us to get in touch with the dynamism of our own relational life in order to deepen and to grow. He does not try to analyze the different stages of the spiritual life. He only attempts to signal cutting edges of his own and to share what has been helpful to him by owning these issues as his own.

Nouwen is a contemplative critic of the values of North American society. His books are a constant and persistent plea for counter-cultural "habits of the heart."[33] He does not insist that we change, since he realizes how hard it is for him to change himself. He suggests rather that we accept ourselves as we are and allow God to transform us in the circumstances of our daily lives. In particular, he calls to conversion those of us who serve the church, keenly aware of how we are tempted to be relevant, popular, and powerful.[34]

As frequent guest lecturer at Regis College, the Jesuit School of Theology in Toronto, his habit is to begin and end with prayer, taking a Scripture passage, using not just the words but also the body-language of standing, gesturing, pacing, pausing, and eye contact. He invites questions and comments, taking the trouble to jot them down, finding out the name of each questioner and clarifying the question, if necessary. He has the gift of making his experience accessible not in a purely subjective way that could be embarrassing, but in a personal way that is evocative of a fuller response to our own process of conversion.

He challenges us to be open to the process of our affective conversion by sharing with us his own. He invites us to get to know ourselves by telling us about his own growth in and resistance to self-knowledge. He shows how a sense of mission springs from conversion by conveying to us his personal convictions about his priestly mission in the church. These convictions have been strengthened by prayer and broadened by his service to God's people.

Conclusion

In this chapter, I have taken three approaches to Nouwen as a prophet of conversion: taking his own life as a paradigm of five insights into conversion, giving examples of these insights in his writings, and describing his pedagogy as another paradigm of these insights. I have tried to show how Nouwen invites us to be open to the process of conversion and to seek out solitude as the place of our turning to God; how he views ministry as a means, not a threat, to our growth in our relationship with God; how he calls us to know our identity in God and our need to share faith with others; and finally how he enables us to live our mission, recognizing the global implications of living in a world-church in solidarity with people who are poor and oppressed.

As one rereads his books and articles in the sequence in which Nouwen wrote them, one can see a growth in his personal relationship with Christ.[35] His willingness to share his own search has opened many others to conversion.[36]

Nouwen finds God in experiences of grace that are not always consoling, like disappointment, the need for reconciliation, and separation. His is a mysticism of everyday life. He experiences God in his changing moods and feelings, in the demands and delights of relationship, and in the concerns of fellow members of the global village. His image of the wounded healer is that of a person with a pierced heart.[37]

There are aspects of contemplative prayer on which Nouwen does not dwell directly — closeness to our bodies, leisure, and creativity. At the same time, however, he draws us into his own experience through his journal style of writing, his exposés of doubts and fears that get as petty and painful as our own, his keen desire and ability to experience God wherever he goes in whatever he is doing, and his ability to articulate his religious experience in ways that are accessible to adult Christians living in the twentieth century.

Nouwen is a prophet of conversion because he is perpetually anxious about his own growth in faith, hope, and love. He assumes that we share his eagerness to improve. His willingness to name, own, and accept his disordered affections can free us to do likewise.

A man of prayer, he knows that the power of Christ can act through his weakness. He turns to God at the beginning of a lecture, takes time for silent prayer while presiding at the Eucharist, and knows himself to be constantly in need of prayer. No doubt what he has learned about life, he has learned in prayer.

He is a man of God for today's world. Keenly aware of his frailties and failures, he lets the Spirit shed light on his mistakes and empower him to speak. He is in tune with the timeless disciplines of the Christian tradition, and applies them realistically to our technological age. Haunted by the destitution of Latin Americans, he opens our eyes to our responsibility to share their burden and to learn from them the joy of gratitude.

Henri Nouwen is a spiritual guide for today. He is steeped in the riches of Christian spirituality and is comfortable urging us to be poor in spirit. Through his meditations on Scripture, he brings the word of God alive showing us how to let the gospel speak to our lives. As one trained in psychology, he balances his awareness of the dynamics of the human psyche with his openness to the workings of the Spirit. As a theologian, he articulates faith seeking understanding in language that appeals to North American Christians. His call to conversion becomes a call to our conversion: his faith story lessens our ambivalence and confirms our desire to deepen our relationship with God.

READINGS

For an overview of Nouwen's approach to the spiritual life, begin with *Reaching Out: The Three Movements of the Spiritual Life* (Garden City, N.Y.: Doubleday, 1975). For an introduction to his approach to pastoral ministry, read *The Wounded Healer: Ministry in Contemporary Society* (Garden City, N.Y.: Doubleday, 1972).

The two books he wrote at the Trappist monastery of the Genesee are *Genesee Diary: Report from a Trappist Monastery* (Garden City, N.Y.: Doubleday, 1976) and *A Cry for Mercy: Prayers from the Genesee* (Garden City, N.Y.: Doubleday, 1981).

The journal that records his time in South America is *Gracias! A Latin American Journal* (San Francisco: Harper & Row, 1983). *In the Name of Jesus: Reflections on Christian Leadership* (New York: Crossroad, 1989) invites the reader to shift values from competitive ambition to contemplative guidance in the Spirit.

For a helpful selection of his writings, see *Seeds of Hope: A Henri Nouwen Reader*, ed. Robert Durback (New York: Bantam, 1989). For an exploration of his spirituality of the heart, see Annice Callahan, "Henri Nouwen: The Heart as Home," in *Spiritualities of the Heart: Approaches to Personal Wholeness in Christian Tradition*, ed. Annice Callahan (New York: Paulist, 1990).

Epilogue

Christianity in a nuclear age can look to these six writers as spiritual guides for today. In her or his own way, each one has translated self-transcendence to mean neither individualism nor escapism, but rather solidarity with the poor and communion among believers.[1]

Evelyn Underhill visited the poor in the Kensington slums twice a week and urged her spiritual directees to engage in some form of volunteer work. She entered into the East-West dialogue by participating in the movement for reconciliation between the Orthodox Church and the Anglican Church, and in the movement for the reunion of churches. Her membership in the Anglican Peace Fellowship at the end of her life is another example of her efforts at global and political self-transcendence.

After becoming a Roman Catholic, Dorothy Day co-founded the Catholic Worker movement to serve poor and unemployed men. This movement inaugurated retreats for its staff members to build a community of shared faith. Her commitment to table fellowship was a living witness to her desire to build communion. Her absolute and consistent pacifism led her to join sit-down strikes, to refuse to comply with the New York City air-raid drills, and to join the women's peace pilgrimage to Rome.

Karl Rahner gave his life for the intellectually poor, believers and unbelievers starved for meaning. His books and lectures were directed largely at intelligent Christians looking for answers to their questions about the faith. He had a special love for university students struggling to make sense of traditional beliefs in a technological era. He also had a special love for atheists and unbelievers since he valued their love of neighbor, their readiness for death, and their hope for the future. He did much to facilitate unity in the Catholic Church and among the Christian churches. Toward the end of his life, he became vocal in support of nuclear disarmament.

Simone Weil stands out for her efforts to bridge the gap between her ideals and reality. Having initially taken a year's leave of absence from her teaching, she spent time as a factory worker, then on a farm. Her struggle for peace led her to fight in the Spanish civil war and then to work with the Free French in London to help her people in occupied France during World War II. Remaining a Jew, she built communion with unbelievers; believing in Christ's real presence in the Eucharist, she hungered for sacramental communion with other Christians. Her choice to eat no more in England than people could eat on war rations in France was the final gesture of solidarity, which led to her eventual death.

Thomas Merton worked in Harlem with the poor before entering the Trappists. His multiple writings on nonviolent resistance testify to his pacifist stance. His letters, books, and lectures reveal his efforts to build communion with Protestants, Buddhists, Hindus, and Sufis. He strengthened the East-West dialogue among monks.

At one time, Henri Nouwen considered moving to Latin America. After making several trips there of varying lengths of time, he realized he was called to live in North America and continue to raise a prophetic voice pointing others to the plight of Latin America. His choice to live with the handicapped at l'Arche is a living reminder of his solidarity with the poor. His books, lectures, and articles continue to build communion among Christians.

These six writers are examples of "noisy contemplation" whereby we celebrate God's presence in ourselves, in others, and in the world, and work for the nonviolent and compassionate alleviation of suffering.[2] They are "manifestations of grace" revealing many faces of God.[3] They are spiritual guides for today, opening our hearts in fresh ways to the Spirit of God.

Notes

Introduction

CW   *Catholic Worker*

Day   William D. Miller, *Dorothy Day: A Biography* (San Francisco: Harper & Row, 1982).

Loneliness   Dorothy Day, *The Long Loneliness* (San Francisco: Harper & Row, 1981).

Mysticism   Evelyn Underhill, *Mysticism: A Study of the Nature and Development of Man's Spiritual Consciousness* (New York: E. P. Dutton & Co., 1961).

Oppression   Simone Weil, "Reflections Concerning the Causes of Liberty and Oppression," *Oppression and Liberty* (London: Routledge & Kegan Paul, 1958).

Writings   Simone Weil, *Formative Writings 1929–1941*, ed. and trans. Dorothy Tuck McFarland and Wilhelmina Van Ness (Amherst: University of Massachusetts Press, 1987).

1. See William D. Miller, *All Is Grace: The Spirituality of Dorothy Day* (Garden City, N.Y.: Doubleday, 1987), 149; Miller, *Harsh and Dreadful Love* (New York: Liveright, 1973), 138–53, 182; Margaret Quigley and Michael Garvey, eds., *The Dorothy Day Book* (Springfield, Ill.: Templegate, 1982), 11, 27, 33, 106, 108.

2. See James Forest, "Waking from a Dream: Thomas Merton and the Catholic Worker," *Catholic Worker* 55 (December 1988): 1, 8.

3. See Thomas Merton, *The Hidden Ground of Love: The Letters of Thomas Merton on Religious Experience and Social Concerns*, ed. William H. Shannon (New York: Farrar, Straus & Giroux, 1985), 136–54.

4. Gordon Zahn, Introduction, *Thomas Merton on Peace* (New York: McCall, 1971), xviii.

5. See Edward Rice, *The Man in the Sycamore Tree: The Good Times and Hard Life of Thomas Merton* (Garden City, N.Y.: Doubleday, Image, 1970), 124.

6. See Dorothy Day, "Thomas Merton, Trappist: 1915–1968," *CW* 34 (December 1968): 1, 6. Reprinted in *Catholic Mind* 67 (February 1969): 32.

7. See Dorothy Day, "Pope John XXIII: The Papacy and World Peace," *American Dialogue* 1 (July-August 1964): 8-10.

8. Thomas Merton, "Pacifism and Resistance in Simone Weil," *Faith and Violence: Christian Teaching and Christian Practice* (Notre Dame: University of Notre Dame Press, 1968), 77; see also 76-84. See also Thomas Merton, *A Vow of Conversation: Journals 1964-1965*, ed. Naomi Burton Stone (New York: Farrar, Straus & Giroux, 1988), 156-60.

9. James Baker, *Thomas Merton, Social Critic* (Lexington, Ky.: University Press of Kentucky, 1971), 116.

10. See Thomas Merton, "Monk in the Diaspora," *Commonweal* 79 (March 20, 1964): 741-45.

11. See Thomas Merton, *Seeds of Destruction* (New York: Farrar, Straus & Giroux, 1964), 93-234, esp. 184-220.

12. See Henri Nouwen, *The Genesee Diary: Report from a Trappist Monastery* (Garden City, N.Y.: Doubleday, 1976), 154-55.

13. See Marc Ellis, *A Year at the Catholic Worker* (New York: Paulist, 1978), 62.

14. Henri Nouwen, *Pray to Live: Thomas Merton, A Contemplative Critic* (Notre Dame: Fides, 1972), 14.

15. See Nouwen, *Genesee Diary*, 84; and Thomas Merton, *Disputed Questions* (New York: Farrar, Straus & Cudahy, 1960), 3-67.

16. See Nouwen, *Genesee Diary*, 87-88; and Thomas Merton, *Conjectures of a Guilty Bystander* (Garden City, N.Y.: Doubleday, 1966), 140-42.

17. See Nouwen, *Genesee Diary*, 160-61, 176.

18. See Nouwen, *Clowning in Rome: Reflections on Solitude, Celibacy, Prayer, and Contemplation* (Garden City, N.Y.: Doubleday, Image, 1979), 88-89.

19. See Evelyn Underhill, *The Mount of Purification* (London: Longmans, Green & Co., 1960), 238-39.

20. For example, see *The Letters of Evelyn Underhill* (Westminster, Md.: Christian Classics, 1989), 175, 313; and Karl Rahner, *Belief Today: Theological Meditations*, ed. Hans Küng (New York: Sheed & Ward, 1967), 25.

21. See Evelyn Underhill, *Ruysbroeck* (London: G. Bell & Sons, 1914), 52-54; and Karl Rahner, *Encounters with Silence*, trans. James M. Demske, S.J. (Westminster, Md.: Newman Press, 1963), 50-51.

22. See Anne Saword, "A Nun's Tribute," in *Thomas Merton/Monk: A Monastic Tribute*, ed. Patrick Hart, O.C.S.O. (New York: Sheed & Ward, 1974), 201-2.

23. See Donald Grayston, *Thomas Merton: The Development of a Spiritual Theologian* (New York: Edwin Mellen Press, 1955), 35-160.

24. For example, see Dorothy Day, Editorials in the *Catholic Worker*, 1933-1980; and Simone Weil, "Reflections concerning the Causes of Liberty and Oppression," *Oppression*, 37-124.

25. See also *Writings*, 91, 99-100, 107-8, 112-13, 134, 151-52.

26. For example, see Simone Weil, "Reflections Concerning the Causes of Liberty and Social Oppression," *Oppression*, 37-124; "On the Contradictions of Marxism," *Oppression*, 147-55; "Fragments, London, 1943," *Oppression*, 156-68; "Is There a Marxist Doctrine?" *Oppression*, 169-95.

27. See *Loneliness*, 133, 142, 145, 161; and Weil, *Seventy Letters: Some Hitherto Untranslated Texts from Published and Unpublished Sources*, trans. Richard Rees (New York: Oxford University Press, 1965), 80–81.

28. See Dorothy Day, *On Pilgrimage: The Sixties* (New York: Curtis Books, 1972).

29. See Thomas Merton, *Contemplative Prayer* (Garden City, N.Y.: Doubleday, Image, 1971), 86–87.

30. See Robert Kress, "Thomas Merton and Karl Rahner: Mystics for Modern Man," *Drew Gateway* 50 (1980): 46–51.

1. EVELYN UNDERHILL
Pathfinder for Our Way to God

Abba	Evelyn Underhill, *Abba: Meditations on the Lord's Prayer* (London: Longmans, Green & Co., 1940).
Adornment	Evelyn Underhill, Introduction, John of Ruysbroeck, *The Adornment of the Spiritual Marriage*, trans. Dom C. A. Wynschenk (London: John M. Watkins, 1951).
Cropper	Margaret Cropper, *Life of Evelyn Underhill* (New York: Harper & Bros., 1958).
Essentials	Evelyn Underhill, *The Essentials of Mysticism and Other Essays* (New York: E. P. Dutton & Co., 1960).
EU-Brame	Evelyn Underhill, *The Ways of the Spirit*, ed. Grace Adolphsen Brame (New York: Crossroad, 1990).
EU-Greene	Dana Greene, ed., Introduction, *Evelyn Underhill: Modern Guide to the Ancient Quest for the Holy* (Albany, N.Y.: State University of New York Press, 1988).
Fruits	Evelyn Underhill, *The Fruits of the Spirit* (London: Longmans, Green & Co., 1945), 7–43.
House	Evelyn Underhill, *The House of the Soul and Concerning the Inner Life* (Minneapolis: Seabury Press, 1984), 107.
Kabir	See *One Hundred Poems of Kabir* trans. Rabindranath Tagore assisted by Evelyn Underhill (London: Macmillan Co., 1915).
Letters	Evelyn Underhill, *The Letters of Evelyn Underhill*, ed. Charles Williams (Westminster, Md.: Christian Classics, 1989).
Life	Evelyn Underhill, *The Life of the Spirit and the Life of Today* (San Francisco: Harper & Row, 1986).

Light   Evelyn Underhill, *Light of Christ* (Toronto: Longmans, Green
                 & Co., 1944).

Man   Evelyn Underhill, *Man and the Supernatural* (New York:
                 E. P. Dutton & Co., 1927), 21.

Meditations   Evelyn Underhill, *Meditations and Prayers* (London: Long-
                 mans, Green & Co., 1944).

Mixed   Evelyn Underhill, *Mixed Pasture: Twelve Essays and Ad-
                 dresses* (London: Methuen & Co., 1933).

Mount   Evelyn Underhill, *The Mount of Purification* (London: Long-
                 mans, Green & Co., 1960).

Mystery   Evelyn Underhill, *The Mystery of Sacrifice: A Meditation on
                 the Liturgy* (London: Longmans, Green & Co., 1948).

Mystic Way   Evelyn Underhill, *The Mystic Way: A Psychological Study in
                 Christian Origins* (Folcroft, Pa.: Folcroft Library Editions,
                 1975).

Mysticism   Evelyn Underhill, *Mysticism: A Study of the Nature and De-
                 velopment of Man's Spiritual Consciousness* (New York: E. P.
                 Dutton & Co. 1961).

Mystics   Evelyn Underhill, *The Mystics of the Church* (New York:
                 Schocken Books, 1964).

Path   John Cordelier, *The Path of the Eternal Wisdom: A Mysti-
                 cal Commentary on the Way of the Cross*, 6th ed. (London:
                 John M. Watkins, 1948).

Practical   Evelyn Underhill, *Practical Mysticism: A Little Book for
                 Normal People* (New York: E. P. Dutton & Co., 1915).

School   Evelyn Underhill, *The School of Charity: Meditations on the
                 Christian Creed* (Toronto: Longmans, Green & Co., 1934).

Sequence   Evelyn Underhill, *The Golden Sequence: A Fourfold Study of
                 the Spiritual Life* (London: Methuen & Co., 1932).

Spiral Way   John Cordelier, *The Spiral Way, Being Meditations upon
                 the Fifteen Mysteries of the Soul's Ascent* (London: John M.
                 Watkins, 1922).

Spiritual Life   Evelyn Underhill, *The Spiritual Life* (London: Mowbray,
                 1955), 11.

   1. See also Joy Marie Milos, C.S.J., "The Role of the Spiritual Guide in
the Life and Writings of Evelyn Underhill," Dissertation, Catholic University
of America, 1988, 69, which regards this book as "a pioneering study of the
question of the universality of religious experience."

2. See *Mysticism* 81–94. Cf. William James, *Varieties of Religious Experience* (London: Gifford Lectures, 1902), 292–93, in which he delineates ineffability, noetic quality, transiency, and passivity as the four marks of the mystic state. See also Grace Adolphsen Brame, "Divine Grace and Human Will in the Writings of Evelyn Underhill," Dissertation, Temple University, 1988, viii–xviii.

3. See *Mysticism*, 94–148, 168, 198–297, 358–443

4. Regarding the authorship of the Pauline epistles, she followed the example of the majority of critics in her day by considering Colossians and Ephesians Pauline, but questioning the authenticity of the epistles to Timothy and Titus. See *Mystic Way*, 159, n. 1. She adopted Ramsay's chronology of Paul's life, aware that Sabatier and others disagreed (*Mystic Way*, 165, n. 2). She indicated her awareness that Pauline scholars dispute the meaning of Paul's "thorn in the flesh" (*Mystic Way*, 176–77, n. 3). Along with other scholars, she questioned the authorship of the Gospel of John (*Mystic Way*, 217, n. 1).

She had a knowledge of Latin, German, French, Italian, and Spanish, and read the writings of the mystics in the original whenever possible (*Mystic Way*, 236–37, n. 2; 248, n. 1; 325, n. 2).

5. See *Practical*, 2–3, 9, 12, 17, 19, 20–21, 22, 37, 124, 103–4. Cf. Annice Callahan, R.S.C.J., "Creative Intuition as Analogous to Contemplative Intuition," *RSCJ: A Journal of Reflection* 2 (1980): 77–88.

6. See Evelyn Underhill, *Ruysbroeck* (London: G. Bell & Sons, 1914), 52–54.

7. See Evelyn Underhill, "The Future of Mysticism," in EU-Greene, 63, 65, 72, 75, 78. Cf. EU-Brame, "Divine Grace and Human Will in the Writings of Evelyn Underhill," 234–67.

8. It is significant that in 1906 Underhill published a book called *The Miracles of Our Lady Saint Mary* (New York: E. P. Dutton & Co., 1906), which is a collection of folk tales about Mary, the Mother of God. In 1922, she published a book of meditations on the Rosary under the pseudonym of John Cordelier. In it she called Mary the Mother of God a pathfinder for our "self-mergence in Christ" and a thoroughfare of the divine life. See *Spiral Way*, 14, 153, 169. For Underhill, Mary is a model of how to follow the spiral way that links the human and the divine (*Spiral Way*, 162, 175). Again, in *The Path of the Eternal Wisdom*, Underhill calls Mary "one of ourselves" since she is *our* Lady, humanity's contribution to the eternal plan. See *Path*, 55. In climbing the mount of purification, we can take Mary, the Mother of God, as an example on each terrace since she is the classical pattern of every human being turned to God. See *Mount*, 13. Underhill wrote frequently of shrines to Mary in *Shrines and Cities of France and Italy*, ed. Lucy Menzies (London: Longmans, Green & Co., 1949), 62, 67, 76, 87, 96–97, 102, 105, 108, 114–15, 117–18.

9. See *Mystic Way*, 64–65, 115, 122, 144, 192, 302, 329.

10. See Evelyn Underhill, *Jacopone da Todi: Poet and Mystic 1228–1306. A Spiritual Biography* (Toronto: J. M. Dent & Sons, 1919). Cf. Mary Xavier Kirby, S.S.J., "The Writings of Evelyn Underhill: A Critical Analysis," dissertation, University of Pennsylvania, 1965, 248, 262–73, 275–77.

11. See *Essentials*, 151, 172, 196, 205, 226, 237.

12. Evelyn Underhill, Introduction, François Malaval, *A Simple Method of*

Raising the Soul to Contemplation in the Form of a Dialogue, trans. Lucy Menzies (London: J. M. Dent & Sons, 1931), xiii.

13. See Evelyn Underhill, ed., Introduction, *A Book of Contemplation, the Which Is Called the Cloud of Unknowing, in the Which a Soul Is Oned with God,* 4th ed. (London: John M. Watkins, 1946), 13-14.

14. See Evelyn Underhill, ed., Introduction, Walter Hilton, *The Scale of Perfection* (London: John M. Watkins, 1948), xlii. Cf. David Knowles, *The English Mystical Tradition* (London: Burns & Oates, 1961), 101, n. 2, 103.

15. See Underhill, Introduction, Richard Rolle, *The Fire of Love or Melody of Love and the Mending of Life or Rule of Living,* ed. Frances M. M. Comper (London: Methuen & Co., 1914), vii-viii.

16. See Underhill, *Adornment,* xi-xxxii. In her introduction, she indicated that she had a certain familiarity with Flemish since she was able to translate certain of his favorite expressions directly. See *Adornment,* xi-xxxii, xxiv, xxv, xxviii, xxix, and xxx. Cf. Kirby, "Writings of Evelyn Underhill," 247, 249-62, 273-75.

17. See *Sequence,* vii, 32-35, 39, 55, 58, 78, 98-99, 100, 104, 111, 114-15, 118-19, 123, 133, 170. See also *Letters,* 216, 218, 231, 233, 235, 243, 245, 299, 306, 307, 318. Cf. Kirby, "Writings of Evelyn Underhill," 55-56, 136-37, 228-29, 260, 272-73, 318.

18. On the centrality of love, see Evelyn Underhill, *The Column of Dust* (London: Methuen & Co., 1909), 2, 164-65, 225, 229, 275-76, 304; *The Grey World* (London: William Heinemann, 1904), 137, 306-7; *The Lost Word* (London: William Heinemann, 1907); and *Theophanies: A Book of Verse* (New York: E. P. Dutton & Co., 1916), 3-4, 62-63.

On the image of Martha and Mary, see *The Grey World,* 18; *Immanence: A Book of Verses* (London: J. M. Dent & Sons, 1913), 77; and *The Lost Word,* 4.

On the incorporation of the homey into one's experience of the transcendent, see *Column of Dust,* 79; *The Grey World,* 50, 74, 129, 162, 260; *Immanence,* 1-2; *The Lost Word,* 217, 316; and *Theophanies,* 9-11, 13, 38, 64, 111, 115-16.

On life according to the mystic way, see *Column of Dust,* 87-88; *The Grey World,* 229, 314; *The Lost Word,* 293-301, 309-16; and *Theophanies,* 1, 41-43, 67-69, 81-83, 90-92.

On the metaphor of God as beauty, see *The Grey World,* 84, 198, 218, 319; *Immanence,* 4-10, 58; and *The Lost Word,* 307. Cf. Charles Gardner, *In Defence of the Faith* (Oxford: Basil Blackwell, 1927), 71.

On the mystical experience of the real presence of Christ, see *Column of Dust,* 138-39, 154, 301; and *The Grey World,* 195-96.

On the symbol of Mary as mother of God, see *A Bar-Lamb's Ballad Book* (London: Kegan Paul, Trench Truebner & Co., 1902), 32-33; *Column of Dust,* 79, 276; *The Grey World,* 195, 217-19, 296-97, 304; *Immanence,* 36, 40-41, 49-51; *The Lost Word,* 164-76, 222-25, 247, 281, 291-94; and *The Miracles of Our Lady Saint Mary.*

On the value of redemptive suffering, see *Column of Dust,* 194, 225; *Immanence,* 70-71, 81; *The Lost Word,* 287-301, 315; and *Theophanies,* 5-8, 75-77.

19. On the image of Martha and Mary, see *Life*, 218; *House*, 46, 60; *Mixed*, 14-15, 19, 74-75, 83, 117; *Meditations*, 8; *Mount*, 9; *Letters*, 90-92.

On the incorporation of the homey into one's experience of the transcendent, see *Spiral Way*, 15, 34, 49, 54, 64, 84, 108, 115, 157; *Life*, xviii, 24, 124; *Man*, 41, 51, 74, 76-107, 113-14, 122-23, 128-30, 142, 167, 198; EU-Brame, 99, 112, 114, 121, 127, 130, 152, 173, 184, 186, 195, 210, 215, 219, 228, 230-31; *House*, 3, 4, 6, 17, 27, 29, 35, 50, 53, 56; *Sequence*, 11, 116, 122, 125, 136, 138, 148, 155, 158, 166, 191-92; *Mixed*, 163-65; *School*, 6, 10, 11, 17, 40-41, 67; *Worship* (New York: Harper & Brothers, 1937), 70, 75, 122, 151, 153, 173, 193-253, 318-19; *Mystery*, xi, xii, xvii, 10, 16, 18, 21, 23, 65; *Abba*, 8, 16, 31, 37, 41, 51, 58; *Light*, 36, 50, 92, 97; *Meditations*, 14, 18, 19, 25, 26, 28, 37, 57, 60; Introduction, Henri de Tourville, *Letters of Direction: Thoughts on the Spiritual Life from the Letters of the Abbé de Tourville*, trans. Lucy Menzies (Westminster: Dacre Press, 1954), 7, 9, 10; and *Letters*, 215.

20. See *House*, 8. On this metaphor, see also her references to its use by Augustine and Teresa of Avila, *House*, 3, 6, 8, 10.

21. See *Letters*, 174, 217-18, 220, 223-26, 238, 241, 252, 265, 287, 293, 313, 320, 338.

22. See *Spiritual Life*, 15-17, 20-22, 24-25, 30, 33, 35, 55.

23. *Letters*, 64. Cf. *Letters*, 224, 236-37, 242, 244, 250, 317, 340.

24. See Evelyn Underhill, *Worship* (San Francisco: Harper & Brothers, 1937), 3, 47, 186, 339.

25. See *Life*, 121-22, 128-29, 135, 144, 171, 206-7, 217.

26. *Letters*, 261, 312. She chose and arranged a collection of eucharistic prayers from ancient liturgies. She demonstrated her familiarity with a wide range of material by drawing not only on the Roman and Gallican rites of the Western church, but also the rites of the west Syrian church, the Egyptian church, and the Byzantine liturgies. See *Eucharistic Prayers from the Ancient Liturgies*, chosen and arranged by Evelyn Underhill (London: Longmans, Green & Co., 1939), 14-16.

27. For references to von Hügel, see Underhill, *Life*, 22, 39, 125-26, 147, 153, 158; *Man*, 15, 26, 33, 37, 53, 70, 87, 99, 100, 147, 155, 168, 203, 231. For references to Christian realism, see *Man*, 106, 183. For references to an incarnational religion, see *Man*, 108-75. See especially the example she gives of Roman Catholic devotion to the Sacred Heart on 141-42.

See also Underhill, *Sequence*, 9, 25-26, 58, 63, 136, 187-88; "Finite and Infinite: A Study of the Philosophy of Baron Friedrich von Hügel" and "Additional Note: Baron von Hügel as a Spiritual Teacher," *Mixed*, 210-34; *Worship*, 12, 15, 349.

She often referred to him in her letters, mentioning his illnesses, recommending his writings, and quoting him to others. See Underhill, *Letters*, 129, 153, 156, 162, 170, 175, 177, 183, 192, 196, 199, 207, 210, 214, 216, 221-25, 230, 232, 234, 237-38, 240, 256-57, 275, 296, 304, 319, 324, 330, 336.

28. On her advice about developing nonreligious interests, see Underhill, *Letters*, 175, 192, 313. On his advice to her on this point, see his November 5, 1921, letter to her in Cropper, 71.

On her advice about getting involved with the poor, see Underhill, *Letters*, 81.

On his advice to her on this point, see his undated letter written after Christmas 1921, in Cropper, 75.

On her advice about participation in church worship, see Underhill, *Letters*, 311. On his advice to her on this point, see his letter of October 29, 1921, in Cropper, 69–70.

29. On her use of the expression "homely," see Cropper, 101. On his use of the word "homely" in his letters to her, see Cropper, 75, 76, 79.

30. See von Hügel's letter to Underhill of October 29, 1921, in Cropper, 69.

31. See his letter to Underhill after Christmas 1921, in Cropper, 77–80.

32. In a letter Underhill compared the process of her growingly personal experience of Christ to watching the sun rise very slowly. She felt that by the end of her life, the Christocentric side nearly predominated. See Cropper, 98, 105, 108. Cf. Underhill in Greene, *Modern Guide*, 9.

After von Hügel's death, she was directed by Don John Chapman, Walter Howard Frere, and then Reginald Somerset Ward. See Christopher J. R. Armstrong, *Evelyn Underhill (1875–1941): An Introduction to Her Life and Writings* (London: Mowbray, 1975), 239–51, regarding Frere and Ward. Cf. Kirby, "Writings of Evelyn Underhill," 30–31, regarding Chapman and Ward.

33. Kirby, "Writings of Evelyn Underhill," 42–48.

34. See Underhill, "Mysticism and War," *The Quest* 6 (January 1915): 207–19, later revised as a pamphlet; and "Problems of Conflict," *Hibbert Journal* 13 (April 1915): 497–510. Cf. James R. Horne, *The Moral Mystic* (Waterloo, Ontario: Wilfrid Laurier University Press, 1983), 77–84.

35. See Cropper, 215. See also Armstrong, *Evelyn Underhill (1875–1941): An Introduction to Her Life and Writings*, 287–89).

36. For her correspondence with E. I. Watkin see *Letters*, 283–85, 200, 305. For her testimony to pacifism, see *Letters*, 253, 262, 283, 286, 288, 299–300, 308, 310. Cf. Dana Greene, "Evelyn Underhill and Her Response to War," *Historical Magazine of the Protestant Episcopal Church* 50 (June 1986), 127–35.

37. On the growing place of social justice in her spirituality, see Terry Tastard, *The Spark in the Soul: Spirituality and Social Justice* (London: Darton, Longman and Todd, 1989), 68–94.

38. See Richard Woods, O.P., ed., *Understanding Mysticism* (Garden City, N.Y.: Doubleday, Image, 1980), 1–15, esp. 2, 3, 11, 13.

39. For example, see Anne Bancroft, "Evelyn Underhill," *Weavers of Wisdom: Women Mystics of the Twentieth Century* (London: Penguin Books, 1989), 82–93.

40. For example, see Karl Rahner, S.J., *Everyday Faith*, trans. W. J. O'Hara (New York: Herder and Herder, 1968); and "Reflections on the Experience of Grace," *Theological Investigations* 3, trans. Karl-H. and Boniface Kruger (New York: Seabury, 1974), 86–90.

41. For example, see K. Rahner, "Reflections on the Unity of the Love of Neighbor and the Love of God," *Theological Investigations* 6, trans. Karl-H. and Boniface Kruger (New York: Seabury, 1974), 231–49; and *The Love of Jesus and the Love of Neighbor*, trans. Robert Barr (New York: Crossroad, 1983).

42. K. Rahner, *Visions and Prophecies*, trans. Charles Henkey and Richard Strachan (New York: Herder and Herder, 1964), 14, n. 12.

43. See K. Rahner, "Religious Enthusiasm and the Experience of Grace," *Theological Investigations* 16, trans. David Morland, O.S.B. (New York: Seabury, Crossroad, 1979), 35–51; and "Mystical Experience and Mystical Theology," *Theological Investigations* 17, trans. Margaret Kohl (New York: Seabury, Crossroad, 1981), 90–99.

44. Karl Rahner, S.J., "Christian Living Formerly and Today," *Theological Investigations* 7, trans. David Bourke (New York: Herder and Herder, 1971), 15. Cf. Harvey D. Egan, S.J., " 'The Devout Christian of the Future Will... Be a "Mystic." ' Mysticism and Karl Rahner's Theology," *Theology and Discovery: Essays in Honor of Karl Rahner, S.J.*, ed. William J. Kelly, S.J. (Milwaukee: Marquette University Press, 1980), 139–58.

45. See Dana Greene, *Evelyn Underhill: Artist of the Infinite Life* (New York: Crossroad, 1990), 144. See also 7 and 150.

46. See Lucy Menzies, "Memoir," *Light of Christ* (Toronto: Longmans, Green & Co., 1944), 20–22.

2. DOROTHY DAY
Peacemaker in Our Nuclear Age

Day	William D. Miller, *Dorothy Day: A Biography* (San Francisco: Harper & Row, 1982).
House	Dorothy Day, *House of Hospitality* (New York: Sheed & Ward, 1939).
Loaves	Dorothy Day, *Loaves and Fishes* (San Francisco: Harper & Row, 1983).
Loneliness	Dorothy Day, *The Long Loneliness: The Autobiography of Dorothy Day* (San Francisco: Harper & Row, 1981).
Pilgrimage	Dorothy Day, *On Pilgrimage* (New York: Catholic Worker Books, 1948).
Sixties	Dorothy Day, *On Pilgrimage: The Sixties* (New York: Curtis Books, 1972).
Union	Dorothy Day, *From Union Square to Rome* (Silver Spring, Md.: Preservation of the Faith Press, 1940).

1. See Dorothy Day, "Having a Baby," *The New Masses* 4 (June 1928): 5–6; and *Loneliness*, 140–61. Robert Coles ascribes their splitting up to "separate inabilities to break faith with themselves," in *A Spectacle Unto the World: The Catholic Worker Movement* (New York: Viking, 1973), 26. On 28–29, Coles speculates that Dorothy's conversion may have been a turning to the church as mother, father, home. After their separation, Forster continued to keep in touch. See *Day*, 326, 342, 349, 357, 360, 369, 387, 390, 421, 457–59, 501, 511, 517. In letters written in 1978 and 1979, Dorothy indicates that Forster phoned

her almost every day. See William D. Miller, *All Is Grace: The Spirituality of Dorothy Day* (Garden City, N.Y.: Doubleday, 1987), 194, 198.

2. For example, *House*, 25, 40, 118, 131, 140, 151, 154, 158-59, 184, 190, 201-2, 216, 241-42, 268. See *Pilgrimage*, 35, 45, 94-95, 153, 175; *Sixties*, 52, 223, 261, 267. Cf. *Day*, 302-3; and Coles, *Dorothy Day: A Radical Devotion*, Radcliffe Biography Series (Reading, Mass: Addison-Wesley, Merloyd Lawrence, 1987), 137, 142.

3. For example, *House*, 25, 71, 74, 117, 131, 135. See *Union*, 152-53, 157, 160, 162, 170; *Pilgrimage*, 13, 18, 42-44, 110, 175; Day, *Therese* (Notre Dame, Ind.: Fides, 1960), vi, 49-50, 106, 151, 174; *Sixties*, 75, 149, 195, 271, 280, 318, 363; Day, Introduction to Brother Lawrence of the Resurrection, *The Practice of the Presence of God*, trans. Donald Attwater (Springfield, Ill.: Templegate, 1974), 7, 9, 19. Cf. Coles, *A Spectacle unto the World*, 33-35; Mel Piehl, *Breaking Bread: The Catholic Worker and the Origin of Catholic Radicalism in America* (Philadelphia: Temple University Press, 1982), 19; Miller, *All Is Grace*, 106, 108, 128, 144, 186; Coles, *Dorothy Day*, 137.

4. For example, *House*, 74, 131; *Pilgrimage*, 147-48, 150, 164-65; *Therese*, esp. 109, where Day observes that little attention has been given to the joys and transports in Thérèse's life that are also part of her little way that is accessible and meant for all of us; *Sixties*, 52, 142, 258, 295; Day, Introduction to *The Practice of the Presence of God*, 12. Another example of Thérèse's ordinariness is her willingness to endure the bitter cold in the convent, just as poor people have to endure bitter cold in certain climates. See Day, *Therese*, 152. Cf. Coles, *A Spectacle Unto the World*, 52-55; Miller, *Day*, 431; Piehl, *Breaking Bread*, 89, n. 7; and Robert Ellsberg, ed., *By Little and By Little: The Selected Writings of Dorothy Day* (New York: Alfred A. Knopf, 1983), xxxiv.

5. See *House*, 23-24, 56, 68-70, 77, 80, 121, 170.

6. See Dorothy Day, "Hell Is Not to Love Anymore," *Catholic Worker* 6 (May 1939): 4; and "On Prayer," unpublished address, Ohio Catholic Education Association, Cincinnati, Ohio, September 30, 1971, Marquette University Archives, audio cassette. See also Ellsberg, *By Little and By Little*, xxxv. Cf. Miller, "Dorothy Day, 1897-1980: All Was Grace," *America* 151 (December 13, 1980): 382-86.

7. *Loneliness*, 71. See also 47-50, 69-71. Cf. *Square*, 51-60. See Karl Rahner, S.J., "Anonymous Christianity and the Missionary Task of the Church," *Theological Investigations* 12, trans. David Bourke (New York: Seabury, 1974), 161-67; "Observations on the Problem of the 'Anonymous Christian,'" *Theological Investigations* 14, trans. David Bourke (New York: Seabury, 1976), 280-94; and *Foundations of Christian Faith: An Introduction to the Idea of Christianity* (New York: Seabury, 1978), 295-98. Cf. Private interview with Professor Rahner on February 25, 1982, in which he used the phrase "anonymous graced one." On tape.

8. See Dorothy Day, *The Eleventh Virgin* (New York: Boni, 1924), 246-311. Cf. Piehl, *Breaking Bread*, 14-15; and Miller, *Day*, 125-57. She needed to make peace with her own past. In a March 1970 conversation with Robert Coles, she said that she was against separating the moral life and public life of a social activist, meaning herself. In particular, she regretted having published her auto-

biographical novel, *The Eleventh Virgin*, and tried to learn from the mistakes she had made. She found it easier to berate herself than to forgive herself for having explored developmentally and experientially what love meant. See Coles, *Dorothy Day*, 34–38.

9. See *House*, 62–63, 97, 222–23, 255–56, 275. On the unity of the love of neighbor and the love of God in her writings, see *Pilgrimage*, 54, 64–55, 99, 125, 166; *Sixties*, 21, 77, 110–11, 209, 330, 359; Day, *Loaves*, 200–204. On finding Christ in others, see Day, *Pilgrimage*, 90, 123, 127, 174; *Sixties*, 22, 77, 97, 168–70, 227, 234–36, 273, 330, 353.

10. For the use of this phrase, I am indebted to Carter Heyward, *Our Passion for Justice: Images of Power, Sexuality, and Liberation* (New York: Pilgrim Press, 1984).

11. On Castro's Cuba, see *Sixties*, 16–19, 68–131, 208. On Martin Luther King and the struggles of black people, see *Sixties*, 149–56, 175, 192–93, 213–20, 225, 335–38. On the peace movement, see *Sixties*, 160–64, 237–39, 254–55, 262, 277, 289–96, 307, 330, 344, 357–61. On César Chávez and the California grape strike, see *Sixties*, 265–66, 293–302, 319, 355, 366–76.

12. See *Loaves*, 210. Cf. Charles J. Healey, S.J., "Dorothy Day (1897–1980)," *Modern Spiritual Writers: Their Legacies of Prayer* (Staten Island, N.Y.: Alba House, 1989), 3–23.

13. See *Houses*, 270–75; "The Roots of Radicalism," an unpublished article written in the early 1960s, *Catholic Worker* 55 (May 1988): 1, 12; and *Loaves*, 78, where she calls inflicted poverty "destitution," reserving the word "poverty" for voluntary poverty. I was struck by the voluntary poverty of those living at Haley House, affiliated with Catholic Worker houses of hospitality in Boston, when I spent a day helping them serve meals on January 27, 1989. Cf. Belden C. Lane, "Precarity and Permanence: Dorothy Day and the Catholic Worker Sense of Place," *Landscapes of the Sacred: Geography and Narrative in American Spirituality* (New York: Paulist, 1988), 161–83, which speaks of situating the unplaced and unsettling the situated.

14. For example, see *House*, 86, 98, 110–11, 117, 120, 130, 170–71, 274–75; *Pilgrimage*, 76, 171; Day, *Therese*, 11; *Sixties*, 76, 195, 260, 357.

15. Dorothy Day, *Therese*, 175. See also *Pilgrimage*, 41; and Introduction, Brother Lawrence of the Resurrection, *The Practice of the Presence of God*, 7–20.

16. See Dorothy Day, "On the Use of Force," *Catholic Worker* 6 (October 1938): 1, 4, 8; and "We Continue Our Christian Pacifist Stand," *Catholic Worker* 9 (January 1942), 1, 4. Cf. Miller, *A Harsh and Dreadful Love* (New York: Liveright, 1973), 3–16, 168–70, 174, 180; and Piehl, *Breaking Bread*, 155–59.

17. See Dorothy Day, "Who Is My Brother's Keeper?" unpublished address, State University of New York, College at Geneseo, October 6, 1966, Marquette University Archives, audio cassette, C-3. Cf. Miller, *A Harsh and Dreadful Love*, 198; *Day*, 437; and Ellsberg, *By Little and By Little*, xxxiii.

18. See Dorothy Day, "The Papacy and World Peace," *American Dialog* 1 (July–August 1964): 8, 10; and "Bread for the Hungry," speech for the Catholic Eucharistic Congress (August 6, 1976), in *Catholic Worker* 42 (September 1976):

1, 5. Cf. Miller, *A Harsh and Dreadful Love*, 154-84, 302, 310; *Day*, 472, 478-49, 486-90, 513; and Piehl, *Breaking Bread*, 189-239.

19. *House*, 2. On Dorothy's writing style, see Stanley Vishnewski, Foreword, Dorothy Day, *Meditations* (New York: Newman Press, 1970), 3; Piehl, *Breaking Bread*, 21; Coles, Introduction, *Loaves*, ix; and Ellsberg, *By Little and By Little*, xii, xvi. On her commitment to the pragmatism of daily life, see Coles, *Dorothy Day*, 111.

20. *House*, 78. On her self-criticism, see Coles, *Dorothy Day*, 34-40, 98-99, 116-17, 122, 129.

21. See Marc Ellis, *A Year at the Catholic Worker* (New York: Paulist, 1978), 113.

22. See Debra Campbell, "The Catholic Earth Mother: Dorothy Day and Women's Power in the Church," *Cross Currents* 33 (Fall 1984): 270-82.

23. See K. Rahner, "The Man with the Pierced Heart," *Servants of the Lord*, trans. Richard Strachan (New York: Herder and Herder, 1968), 107-19; "Reflections on the Experience of Grace," *Theological Investigations* 3, trans. Karl-H. and Boniface Kruger (New York: Seabury, Crossroad, 1974), 86-90; "Reflections on the Unity of the Love of Neighbor and the Love of God," *Theological Investigations* 6, trans. Karl-H. and Boniface Kruger (New York: Seabury, 1974), 231-49; and *Foundations*, 131. Cf. Annice Callahan, R.S.C.J., *Karl Rahner's Spirituality of the Pierced Heart: A Reinterpretation of Devotion to the Sacred Heart* (Lanham, Md.: University Press of America, 1985).

24. See K. Rahner, *Foundations*, 126-33. Cf. Brian O. McDermott, S.J., *What Are They Saying about the Grace of Christ?* (New York: Paulist, 1984), 10, 12-58.

25. See K. Rahner, "The Spirituality of the Church of the Future," *Theological Investigations* 20, trans. Edward Quinn (New York: Crossroad, 1981), 143-53; and *The Shape of the Church to Come*, trans. Edward Quinn (New York: Crossroad, 1983), 91-132.

3. KARL RAHNER
Theologian of Everyday Christian Life

Belief   Karl Rahner, *Belief Today: Theological Meditations*, ed. Hans Küng, trans. Ray and Rosaleen Ockenden (New York: Sheed & Ward, 1967).

Christian Faith Karl Rahner and Karl-Heinz Weger, *Our Christian Faith: Answers for the Future*, trans. Francis McDonagh (New York: Crossroad, 1981).

Commitment   Karl Rahner, *The Christian Commitment: Essays in Pastoral Theology*, trans. Cecily Hastings (New York: Sheed & Ward, 1968).

Dialogue   *Karl Rahner in Dialogue: Conversations and Interviews*

1965–1982, ed. Paul Imhof and Hubert Biallowons, trans. ed. Harvey D. Egan, S.J. (New York: Crossroad, 1986).

Marketplace	Karl Rahner, *Christian in the Marketplace*, trans. Cecily Hastings (New York: Sheed & Ward, 1966).
Opportunities	Karl Rahner, *Opportunities for Faith: Elements of a Modern Spirituality*, trans. Edward Quinn (New York: Seabury, Crossroad, 1974).
Practice	Karl Rahner, *The Practice of Faith: A Handbook of Contemporary Spirituality*, ed. Karl Lehmann and Albert Raffelt (New York: Crossroad, 1986).
Prayer	Karl Rahner, *On Prayer* (Toronto: Paulist, Deus, 1968).
Prayers	Karl Rahner, *Prayers for a Lifetime*, ed. Albert Raffelt (New York: Crossroad, 1984).
Sacraments	Karl Rahner, *Meditations on the Sacraments* (New York: Seabury, Crossroad, 1977).
Servants	Karl Rahner, *Servants of the Lord*, trans. Richard Strachan (New York: Herder & Herder, 1968).
TI 3	Karl Rahner, *Theological Investigations* 3, trans. Karl-H. and Boniface Kruger (London: Darton, Longman & Todd; Baltimore: Helicon Press, 1967).
TI 4	Karl Rahner, *Theological Investigations* 4, trans. Kevin Smyth (London: Darton, Longman & Todd; Baltimore: Helicon Press, 1966).
TI 6	Karl Rahner, *Theological Investigations* 6, trans. Karl-H. and Boniface Kruger (London: Darton, Longman & Todd; Baltimore: Helicon Press, 1969).
TI 7	Karl Rahner, *Theological Investigations* 7, trans. David Bourke (London: Darton, Longman & Todd; New York: Herder and Herder, 1971).
TI 9	Karl Rahner, *Theological Investigations* 9, trans. David Bourke (London: Darton, Longman & Todd; New York: Herder and Herder, 1972).
TI 11	Karl Rahner, *Theological Investigations* 11, trans. David Bourke (London: Darton, Longman & Todd; New York: Seabury Press, 1974).
TI 13	Karl Rahner, *Theological Investigations* 13, trans. David Bourke (London: Darton, Longman & Todd; New York: Seabury Press, 1975).

TI 16   Karl Rahner, *Theological Investigations* 16, trans. David Morland, O.S.B. (London: Darton, Longman & Todd; New York: Seabury Press, 1979).

TI 17   Karl Rahner, *Theological Investigations* 17, trans. Margaret Kohl (London: Darton, Longman & Todd; New York: Crossroad, 1981).

TI 18   Karl Rahner, *Theological Investigations* 18, trans. Edward Quinn (London: Darton, Longman & Todd; New York: Crossroad, 1983).

TI 19   Karl Rahner, *Theological Investigations* 19, trans. Edward Quinn (London: Darton, Longman & Todd; New York: Crossroad, 1983).

TI 20   Karl Rahner, *Theological Investigations* 20, trans. Edward Quinn (London: Darton, Longman & Todd; New York: Crossroad, 1981).

TI 21   Karl Rahner, *Theological Investigations* 21, trans. Hugh M. Riley (London: Darton, Longman & Todd; New York: Crossroad, 1988).

Visions   Karl Rahner, *Visions and Prophecies*, Quaestiones Disputatae 10, trans. Charles Henkey and Richard Strachan (New York: Herder & Herder, 1964).

Wintry   *Faith in a Wintry Season: Conversations and Interviews with Karl Rahner in the Last Years of His Life*, ed. Paul Imhof and Hubert Biallowons, trans. ed. Harvey D. Egan, S.J. (New York: Crossroad, 1990).

1. See *Practice* and *Prayers*. Cf. Dermot Lane, *The Experience of God: An Invitation to Do Theology* (New York: Paulist, 1981), 9–13.
2. See "Reflections on the Experience of Grace," *TI* 3:86–90; "Theology and Anthropology," *TI* 9:28–45; "The Experience of God Today," *TI* 11:149–65; "Experience of Self and Experience of God," *TI* 13:122–132; "Experience of the Holy Spirit," *TI* 18:189–210; *Foundations of Christian Faith: An Introduction to the Idea of Christianity*, trans. William V. Dych, S.J. (New York: Seabury, Crossroad, 1978), 131; "Alltagstugenden," *Geist und Leben* 43 (1970): 46–57; and "Glaubensmitte — Lebensmitte," *Geist und Leben* 46 (1973): 241–46. Cf. Anne Carr, B.V.M., *The Theological Method of Karl Rahner* (Missoula, Mont.: Scholars Press for the American Academy of Religion, 1977), and "Theology and Experience in the Thought of Karl Rahner," *Journal of Religion* 53 (1973): 359–73; J. Norman King, "The Experience of God in the Theology of Karl Rahner," *Thought* 53 (1978): 164–202, and *Experiencing God All Ways and Every Day* (Minneapolis: Winston, 1982); and Brian O. McDermott, S.J., *What Are They Saying about the Grace of Christ?* (New York: Paulist, 1984).

3. See *Opportunities*, 62–73. Cf. Leo J. O'Donovan, S.J., ed., *A World of Grace: An Introduction to the Themes and Foundations of Karl Rahner's Theology* (New York: Seabury, Crossroad, 1980).

4. Professor Rahner made this point with me in a private interview on April 26, 1982. On tape. See Rahner, *Mary Mother of the Lord* (New York: Herder & Herder, 1967), 17, 36–37, 55–56, 60–61.

5. See Karl Rahner, *Ignatius of Loyola*, trans. Rosaleen Ockenden (New York: Collins, 1979), 37–38. On the influence of Ignatian spirituality on Rahner, see *Wintry*, 18–19, 30, 39, 96, 104, 122; and Foreword, *TI* 16:x. Professor Klaus Fischer underlined this point with me in a private interview, July 12, 1982.

6. See Karl Rahner, "What Does Vatican II Teach about Atheism?" *The Pastoral Approach to Atheism*, Concilium 23, ed. Karl Rahner (New York: Paulist, 1967), 7–24; "The Church and Atheism," *TI* 21:137–50.

7. Karl Rahner, "Christian Living Formerly and Today," *TI* 7:15. See also *Everyday Faith*, 76–83; and "The Spirituality of the Church of the Future," *TI* 20:143–153. Cf. Harvey D. Egan, S.J., " 'The Devout Christian of the Future Will... Be a "Mystic." ' Mysticism and Karl Rahner's Theology," ed. William J. Kelly, S.J., *Theology and Discovery: Essays in Honor of Karl Rahner, S.J.* (Milwaukee: Marquette University Press, 1980), 139–58.

8. See also *Visions*, 7–88. Cf. H. D. Egan, "A Contemporary Mystical Theology," *What Are They Saying about Mysticism?* (New York: Paulist, 1982), 98–108.

9. See *Belief*, 13–43; *Commitment*, 105–6; *Everyday Faith*, trans. W. J. O'Hara (New York: Herder & Herder, 1968), 66; *Servants*, 20; *Do You Believe in God?* trans. Richard Strachan (New York: Paulist, 1969), 112–13; *The Priesthood*, 4–15; and *Sacraments*, 25–26.

10. See Karl Rahner, *The Spirit in the Church*, trans. John Griffiths (New York: Seabury, Crossroad, 1979), 1–31; "Christian Living Formerly and Today," *TI* 7:14; "Religious Enthusiasm and the Experience of Grace, " *TI* 16:44–47; "Mystical Experience and Mystical Theology," *TI* 17:90–99; and "Mysticism," *Encyclopedia of Theology: The Concise Sacramentum Mundi*, ed. K. Rahner (New York: Seabury, Crossroad, 1975), 1010–11.

11. See Rahner, "Priest and Poet," *TI* 3:294–317; and "The Theology of the Symbol," *TI* 4:221–52. Cf. Callahan, *Karl Rahner's Spirituality of the Pierced Heart*, 35–37, 43–46, 90–96.

12. See Rahner, "The Eternal Significance of the Humanity of Jesus for our Relationship with God,' *TI* 3:35–46; " 'Behold This Heart!': Preliminaries to a Theology of Devotion to the Sacred Heart," *TI* 3:321–30; "Some Theses for a Theology of Devotion to the Sacred Heart," *TI* 3:331–52; and "The Man with the Pierced Heart," *Servants*, 107–19. Cf. Callahan, *Karl Rahner's Spirituality of the Pierced Heart*, 37, 46–48, 75–77, 90–100; and Donald Gelpi, S.J., "Karl Rahner's Theology of Devotion to the Sacred Heart," *Woodstock Letters* 95 (1966): 405–17.

13. See *Prayer*, 45–55. See also Rahner, *Encounters with Silence*, trans. James M. Demske, S.J. (Westminster, Md.: Newman Press, 1963).

14. See *Prayer*, 18. See also Karl Rahner, *Watch and Pray with Me*, trans. William V. Dych (New York: Herder & Herder, 1966), 9–33.

15. See *Prayer*, 98–109. See also *Watch and Pray with Me*, 37–63.

16. See Karl Rahner: "The Possibility and Necessity of Prayer,"and "Is Prayer Dialogue with God?" *Christian at the Crossroads*, trans. V. Green (New York: Seabury, Crossroad, 1975), 48–69.

17. On devotion to the cross and to the name of Jesus, for example, see Karl Rahner and Marcel Viller, S.J., *Aszese und Mystik in der Väterzeit. Ein Abriss* (Freiburg im Breisgau: Herder, 1939), 295–302. On praying to the saints, see Rahner, "Herz Jesu, Quell des Lebens. Festansprache am Herz-Jesu-Fest 1953," *Korrespondenzblatt PGC* 88 (1953): 9–10; "Prayer to the Saints," *The Courage to Pray*, trans. Sarah O'Brien Twohig (New York: Crossroad, 1981), 29–87; and "One Mediator and Many Mediations," *TI* 9:169–84.

18. See Karl Rahner, "Über das Beten," *Geist und Leben* 45 (1972): 84–98.

19. See Karl Rahner, "Why Does God Allow Us to Suffer?" *TI* 19:194–208; "Öffnung des Herzens," *Frau und Beruf* 4 (1955): 5.

20. See Karl Rahner, *The Religious Life Today*, trans. V. Green (New York: Seabury, Crossroad, 1976), 49–50.

21. See Karl Rahner, *Foundations of Christian Faith: An Introduction to the Idea of Christianity*, trans. William V. Dych, S.J. (New York: Seabury, Crossroad, 1978), 75–81; and "Geheimnis des Herzens," *Geist und Leben* 20 (1947): 161–65.

22. See Karl Rahner, *The Love of Jesus and the Love of Neighbor*, trans. Robert Barr (New York: Crossroad, 1983), 69–104. Cf. King, *Experiencing God*, 73–90.

23. For example, *Opportunities*, 143; *Meditations on Hope and Love* (New York: Crossroad, 1977), 84–85; *Marketplace*, 61–79.

24. Rahner, *The Love of Jesus*, 39. See also 15, and *Foundations of Christian Faith*, 203–6.

25. See Rahner, *The Love of Jesus*, 65–104; and *Dialogue*, 184–185.

26. See Karl Rahner, Foreword, Pedro Arrupe, S.J., *In Him Alone Is Our Hope: Texts on the Heart of Christ 1965–1983*, ed. Jerome Aixala, S.J. (St. Louis: Institute of Jesuit Sources, 1984), xiii. Cf. Callahan, *Karl Rahner's Spirituality of the Pierced Heart*, 112, 130–33; and "The Relationship between Spirituality and Theology," *Horizons* 16 (1989): 266–74.

27. See Rahner, "The Future of the Church and the Church of the Future," *TI* 20:103–14; *The Love of Jesus*, 75–104; and *The Shape of the Church to Come*, trans. Edward Quinn (New York: Crossroad, 1983).

28. See Karl Rahner, *I Remember: An Autobiographical Interview with Meinold Krauss*, trans. Harvey D. Egan, S.J. (New York: Crossroad, 1985), 63–68.

29. See Karl Rahner, *Grace in Freedom*, trans. Hilda Graef (New York: Herder & Herder, 1969), 9–79, 127–81, 203–64.

30. See *Opportunities*, 63, 93–105, 204–22. Rahner was criticized by Johann Metz and Matthew Lamb for disregarding the socio-political dimensions of reality. See Johann Baptist Metz, *Faith in History and Society*, trans. David Smith (New York: Seabury, 1980); and Matthew Lamb, *Solidarity with Victims* (New York: Crossroad, 1982). Some theologians, however, see elements in Rahner's theology that are open to political and liberation theologies. See Mary E. Hines,

The Transformation of Dogma: An Introduction to Karl Rahner on Doctrine (New York: Paulist, 1989), 131–51; and Leo O'Donovan, S.J., "Orthopraxis and Theological Method in Karl Rahner," *Catholic Theological Society of America Proceedings* 35 (1980): 47–65.

31. See Karl Rahner, *Free Speech in the Church* (New York: Sheed & Ward, 1959), 9–50, 53–112; *Theology for Renewal*, 80; *The Church after the Council*, trans. David C. Herron and Rodelinde Albrecht (New York: Herder & Herder, 1966), 37–73; *The Christian of the Future*, trans. W.J. O'Hara (New York: Herder & Herder, 1967), 77–101; *The Theology of Pastoral Action*, Studies in Pastoral Theology 1, trans. W.J. O'Hara (New York: Herder & Herder, 1968), 64–133; *TI* 19:55–138; and "The Spirituality of the Church of the Future," *TI* 20:147–48. Cf. James C. Bacik: "A Spirituality for the Future: Situational and Systematic," *Rising from History: U.S. Catholic Theology Looks to the Future*, ed. Robert J. Daly, S.J. (Lanham, Md.: University Press of America, 1987), 184–91; and Robert Masson, "Spirituality for the Head, Heart, Hands, and Feet: Rahner's Legacy," *Spirituality Today* 36 (1984): 340–54.

32. See Karl Rahner and Pinchas Lapide, *Encountering Jesus — Encountering Judaism: A Dialogue*, trans. Davis Perkins (New York: Crossroad, 1987), 71.

33. See *Wintry*, 80–84, 128–40, 146, 155–58, 184–87.

34. See Rahner, *The Shape of the Church to Come*, 69–70; and *Is Christian Life Possible Today?* trans. Salvator Attanasio (Denville, N.J.: Dimension Books, 1984).

35. For example, see Heinrich Fries and Karl Rahner, *Unity of the Churches: An Actual Possibility*, trans. Ruth and Eric Gritsch (New York: Paulist, 1985).

36. See James J. Bacik, *Apologetics and the Eclipse of Mystery: Mystagogy According to Karl Rahner* (Notre Dame: University of Notre Dame Press, 1980), ix.

37. See Johannes Baptist Metz, "Karl Rahner — ein theologisches Leben: Theologie als mystische Biographie eines Christenmenschen heute," *Stimmen der Zeit* 192 (1974): 305–16.

4. SIMONE WEIL
Witness to Solidarity in Affliction

Essays   Simone Weil, *Selected Essays 1934–1943*, trans. Richard Rees (New York: Oxford University Press, 1962).

FLN   Simone Weil, *First and Last Notebooks*, trans. Richard Rees (New York: Oxford University Press, 1970).

Grace   Simone Weil, *Gravity and Grace*, trans. Emma Craufurd (New York: Routledge & Kegan Paul, 1987).

Intimations   Simone Weil, *Intimations of Christianity among the Ancient Greeks*, ed. and trans. Elisabeth Chase Geissbuhler (London: Routledge and Kegan Paul, 1957).

Letters	Simone Weil, *Seventy Letters: Some hitherto untranslated texts from published and unpublished sources*, trans. Richard Rees (New York: Oxford University Press, 1965).
Liberty	Simone Weil, *Oppression and Liberty*, trans. Arthur Wills and John Petrie (London: Routledge & Kegan Paul 1958).
Love	Simone Weil, *On Science, Necessity, and the Love of God*, ed. Richard Rees (New York: Oxford University Press, 1968).
Notebooks	Simone Weil, *The Notebooks of Simone Weil*, vols. 1 and 2, trans. Arthur Wills (London: Routledge & Kegan Paul, 1976).
Pensées	Simone Weil, *Pensées sans ordre concernant l'amour de Dieu* (Paris: Editions Gallimard, 1962).
Roots	Simone Weil, *The Need for Roots: Prelude to a Declaration of Duties toward Mankind*, trans. Arthur Wills (New York: G. P. Putnam's Sons, 1952).
Waiting	Simone Weil, *Waiting for God*, trans. Emma Craufurd (San Francisco: Harper & Row, 1951).
Writings	Simone Weil, *Formative Writings 1929–1941*, ed. and trans. Dorothy Tuck McFarland and Wilhelmina Van Ness (Amherst: University of Massachusetts Press, 1987).

1. See *Waiting*, 15–20, 64. Cf. Gabriella Fiori, *Simone Weil: An Intellectual Biography*, trans. Joseph R. Berrigan (Athens, Ga.: University of Georgia Press, 1989), 26, 129, 302, 309; Richard Rees, *Simone Weil: A Sketch for a Portrait* (Toronto: Oxford University Press, 1966), 12; and Vernon Sproxton, "Pilgrim of the Absolute," in Simone Weil, *Gateway to God* (Glasgow: Williams Collins Sons, Fontana, 1974), 27.

2. This chapter does not discuss themes and original insights in Weil's writings that have already been treated, such as decreation, uprootedness, the void, her Jewish background, her rooting of Christianity in Greek thought, her critique of orthodox Marxism, and her social and political thought. See Gustave Thibon, Introduction, *Grace*, vii–xxxvii.

On decreation, see Jacques Cabaud, *Simone Weil à New York et à Londres (1942–1943)* (Paris: Plon, 1967), 149–50; Bernard Halda, *L'évolution spirituelle de Simone Weil* (Paris: Beauchesne, 1964), 95–107; Madeline Hamblin, "Simone Weil's Theology of Evil, Love, and the Self-Emptying of God," in Thomas A. Idinopulos and Josephine Z. Knopp, *Mysticism, Nihilism, Feminism: New Critical Essays on the Theology of Simone Weil* (Johnson City, Tenn.: Institute of Social Sciences and Arts, 1984), 39–56; Dorothy Tuck McFarland, *Simone Weil* (New York: Frederick Ungar, 1983), 136–37; Michael Narcy, *Simone Weil: malheur et beauté du monde* (Paris: Editions de Centurion, 1967), 55–89; and Miklos Veto, *La métaphysique religieuse de Simone Weil* (Paris: Librairie philosophique J. Vrin, 1971).

On uprootedness, see Luce Blech-Lidolf, *La pensée philosophique et sociale de Simone Weil* (Berne: Herbert Lang, 1976), 75–89; Betty McLane-Iles,

Uprooting and Integration in the Writings of Simone Weil (New York: Peter Lang, 1987); and Miklos Veto, "Uprootedness and Alienation in Simone Weil," *Blackfriars* (1962): 392.

On the void, see Gaston Kempfner, *La philosophie mystique de Simone Weil* (Paris: La Colombe, 1960), 149–82; and Peter Winch, *Simone Weil: "The Just Balance"* (Cambridge: Cambridge University Press, 1989), 120–32.

On her attitude toward Judaism, see Jacques Cabaud, *L'expérience vécue de Simone Weil* (Paris: Plon, 1957), 236; Robert Coles, "Her Jewishness," *Simone Weil: A Modern Pilgrimage* (Reading, Mass.: Addison-Wesley, Merloyd Lawrence, 1987), 43–62; Marie-Magdeleine Davy, *The Mysticism of Simone Weil*, trans. Cynthia Rowland (Boston: Beacon Press, 1951), 18–21; Marie-Magdeleine Davy, *Simone Weil* (Paris: Editions Universitaires, 1961), 24; Paul Giniewski, *Simone Weil: ou, La haine de soi* (Paris: Berg International, 1978); Josephine Knopp, "The Carnal God: Simone Weil's Anti-Judaic Perspective," in *Mysticism, Nihilism, Feminism*, 117–138; McFarland, *Simone Weil*, 4–6; George A. Panichas, ed., *The Simone Weil Reader* (New York: David McKay, 1977), xxiii–xxvii; Simone Pétrement, *Simone Weil: A Life*, trans. Raymond Rosenthal (New York: Random House, Pantheon, 1976), 245, 390–92, 395, 421, 443–44, 456–57.

On her incorporation of Greek thought into Christianity, see Blech-Ludolf, *La pensée philosophique et sociale de Simone Weil*, 152–204; Halda, *L'évolution spirituelle de Simone Weil*, 95–107; John Hellman, *Simone Weil: An Introduction to Her Thought* (Philadelphia: Fortress Press, 1984), 47–73; Narcy, *Simone Weil: malheur et beauté du monde*, 35–89; McFarland, *Simone Weil*, 118, 127; and Eric O. Springsted, *Christus Mediator: Platonic Mediation in the Thought of Simone Weil* (Chico, Calif.: Scholars Press, 1983).

On her critique of orthodox Marxism, see Lawrence A. Blum and Victor J. Seidler, *A Truer Liberty: Simone Weil and Marxism* (New York: Routledge, Chapman & Hall, 1989).

On her social and political thought, see Mary G. Dietz, *Between the Human and the Divine: The Political Thought of Simone Weil* (Totowa, N.J.: Towman & Littlefield, 1988); G. Fiori, *Simone Weil: An Intellectual Biography*, 255–99; Jim Grote, "Prestige: Simone Weil's Theory of Social Force," *Spirituality Today* 42 (Autumn 1990): 217–32; and Winch, *Simone Weil: "The Just Balance"*, 179–90.

3. See *Waiting*, 117–136; *Pensées*, 85–105; and *Love*, 170–98. Cf. Eric O. Springsted, *Christus Mediator*, 71–83, and *Simone Weil and the Suffering of Love* (Cambridge, Mass.: Cowley, 1986), 17–131.

4. See *FLN*, 70, 81, 103, 120, 140, 213, 300; *Intimations*, 183.

5. She wrote for three papers: one, the organ of the teachers' trade union affiliated with the CGTU, another, a revolutionary syndicalist journal, and a third, a newspaper of the Lyons trade union of construction workers: "Weil was a revolutionary, and she passionately hoped that out of the profound economic crisis afflicting Europe that seemed to signal the decay of the capitalist system and the imminence of proletarian revolution, a truly egalitarian worker democracy would emerge" (*Writings*, 91).

6. *Writings*, 225. See also *Writings*, 171, 203, 213. So committed was she to the plight of the working class that in 1934 she wrote investigating the historical

facts behind the uprising in 1343 and 1345 of wool workers in Florence. See *Essays*, 55-72, 216-18. Cf. Jacques Cabaud, *Simone Weil: A Fellowship in Love* (London: Harvill Press, 1964), 209-12, where he distinguishes suffering from *malheur*, which marks the afflicted one with servitude, self-loathing, and social degradation.

7. Simone Weil had sent Joë Bousquet her Plan for an Organization of Front-Line Nurses, and he had written back an encouraging letter, which she hoped to use as a letter of recommendation for the plan. See *Letters*, 44.

8. *Roots*, 44-78, esp. 53-55. Cf. John M. Dunaway, "The Need for Roots: Weil's Sociopolitical Thought," *Simone Weil* (Boston: Twayne, 1984), 49-73.

9. On Francis of Assisi, see, for example, *Notebooks*, 644; *Waiting*, 65, 160, 198; *Intimations*, 83; *Lectures*, 168, 179, 181; and *FLN*, 83, 150, 261. Cf. Halda, *L'évolution spirituelle de Simone Weil*, 138-39.

On John of the Cross, see, for example, *Notebooks*, 645; *Waiting*, 96-98, 100, 211; *Intimations*, 83, 137, 170; *Letter to a Priest* (New York: G. P. Putnam's Sons, 1954), trans. A. F. Wills, 34-35, 59; and *FLN*, 110, 131-32, 243, 351. Cf. Halda, *L'évolution spirituelle de Simone Weil*, 135-38.

10. See *Liberty*, 20. Cf. Davy, *Simone Weil*, 72-123; and David McLellan, *Simone Weil: Utopian Pessimist* (London: Macmillan, 1989), 67-92.

11. See *Liberty*, 37-103; Weil, "Factory Journal," *Writings*, 155-226; and *Letters*, 10-17. Cf. Springsted, *Christus Mediator*, 13-23.

12. See Blum and Seidler, *A Truer Liberty*, 146-48.

13. See *Roots*, 97, 295-302. For examples of the worker's conscious domination over matter, *FLN*, 16, 27, 35, 37-39, 44-46, 49, 51, 59, 60-61, 84, 96. Cf. Clare B. Fischer, "The Fiery Bridge: Simone Weil's Theology of Work," dissertation, Graduate Theological Union, 1979; and Halda, *L'évolution spirituelle de Simone Weil*, 72-76.

14. See *Liberty*, 46, 59, 60, 64, 67-68, 71-74, 103-19.

15. See *Letters*, 96-102, 158, and *Writings*, 241-78; see also Gustave Thibon in *Grace*, ix, xvii. Cf. Thomas Merton, "Pacifism and Resistance in Simone Weil," *Faith and Violence: Christian Teaching and Christian Practice* (Notre Dame: University of Notre Dame Press, 1968), 76-84.

16. See *Roots*, 96, 215-16, 219. Cf. Pétrement, *Simone Weil: A Life*, 529-31.

17. See *Waiting*, 67-69, 72; *Letters*, 140-42; *La Connaissance surnaturelle* (Paris: Gallimard, 1950), 9-10. Cf. Cabaud, *Fellowship*, 238-41; Dietz, *Between the Human and the Divine*, 21-34, 85-104, 112-30; and Dorothee Sölle, "The Religion of Slaves," in *Suffering*, trans. Everett R. Kalin (Philadelphia: Fortress Press, 1975), 151-78.

18. For a view that presents Weil's mysticism, see Lucy Bregman, "The Barren Fig Tree: Simone Weil and the Problem of Feminine Identity," in *Mysticism, Nihilism, Feminism*, 110-11.

For a view that presents Weil's nihilism, see Susan A. Taubes, "The Absent God," in *Toward a New Christianity: Readings in the Death of God Theology*, ed. Thomas J. J. Altizer (New York: Harcourt, Brace, and World, 1967), 113-16; and Thomas A. Idinopulos, "Necessity and Nihilism in Simone Weil's Vision of God," in *Mysticism, Nihilism, Feminism*, 17-38.

For a description of mystics experiencing God as a personal mystery, in impersonal symbols, and as both intimate and infinite, see Evelyn Underhill, *Ruysbroeck* (London: G. Bell & Sons, 1914), 52–54.

19. *Letters*, 140. Cf. Hellman, *Simone Weil: An Introduction to Her Thought*, 82–89.

20. See Weil, *Ecrits de Londres et dernières lettres* (Paris: Gallimard, 1957), 160, 177.

21. See Weil, *Ecrits de Londres*, 47, 166–67; *Attente de Dieu* (Paris: Fayard, 1966), 189; *La Connaissance surnaturelle*, 91; *FLN*, 141, 312.

22. Cf. Hellman, *Simone Weil: An Introduction to Her Thought*, 90–97, where he calls them "the three secret presences of God."

23. See Weil, Letter to Solange Beaumier, Casablanca, May 1942, in Joseph-Marie Perrin, *Mon Dialogue avec Simone Weil* (Paris: Nouvelle Cité, 1984), 177.

24. See Weil, *Letter to a Priest*, 19, 31–32, 46, 52, 56, 60, 65, 69. For example, Simone Weil argued forcefully against the notion of a personal Providence that claims a personal and particular intervention by God in human affairs, since it is incompatible with true faith and with a scientific conception of the world. Opposed to a Roman conception of God as a Roman magnate ordering his slaves around and intervening in events in order to be in control, she reverences the sacred as the mystery at the heart of life by holding a conception of an impersonal Providence that lets the sun rise on the good and the evil. She believed in the nonintervention of God in the universe. She viewed Providence as the regulating principle, the order of the world. See *Roots*, 262–85. See also *Waiting*, 26–27; "Dernier texte," *Pensées*, 149–58; *Gateway to God*, 72–74.

Cf. David Anderson, *Simone Weil* (London: SCM Press, 1971), 13–19; Cabaud, *Fellowship in Love*, 242–51, 268–73, 280, 289–94; Coles, "A Radical Grace," *Simone Weil*, 111–33; Davy, *The Mysticism of Simone Weil*, 43–46, 58; Perrin, *Mon Dialogue avec Simone Weil*; Joseph-Marie Perrin, ed., *Réponses aux questions de Simone Weil* (Paris: Montaigue, 1963); Joseph-Marie Perrin and Thibon, *Simone Weil telle que nous l'avons connue* (Paris: Fayard, 1967); Pétrement, *Simone Weil: A Life*, 215–16, 290, 304, 307, 329–30, 333, 339, 363–65, 373, 394, 412, 417–19, 442–47, 450–52, 456–60, 465–66, 469–71, 478–85, 518–19, 523–24; Rees, *A Sketch for a Portrait*, pp. 116–28; Springsted, *Christus Mediator*, pp. 236–39.

25. *Waiting*, 96. See also 151, 163, 193. Cf. Cabaud, *Fellowship in Love*, 241, 259; and Judith Van Herik, "Looking, Eating, and Waiting in Simone Weil," in *Mysticism, Nihilism, Feminism*, 72, 77–80. In "A Radical Grace," in *Simone Weil*, 119, Robert Coles claims: "I think it is fair to say that she fell in love with Jesus; that he became her beloved; that she kept him on her mind and in her heart."

26. See J. Pat Little, *Simone Weil: Waiting on Truth* (New York: Berg, 1988), 122.

27. Richard Rees in *Letters*, 143.

28. For a view in favor of her having been a victim of anorexia nervosa, see Springsted, *Simone Weil and the Suffering of Love*, 6. Cf. Rudolph M. Bell, *Holy Anorexia* (Chicago: University of Chicago Press, 1985).

For views that refute this position, see Bregman, "The Barren Fig Tree," in

Mysticism, Nihilism, Feminism, 101-2; Jacques Cabaud, *Simone Weil* (London: Harvill Press, 1964), 336; Coles, "Her Hunger," in *Simone Weil*, 23-41; Judith van Herik, "Looking, Eating, and Waiting," in *Mysticism, Nihilism, Feminism*, 81-86; Judith Van Herik, "Simone Weil's Religious Imagery: How Looking Becomes Eating," in *Immaculate and Powerful: The Female in Sacred Image and Social Reality*, ed. Clarissa Atkinson et al. (Boston: Beacon Press, 1985), 260-82; and Pétrement, *Simone Weil: A Life*, 215, 420-41, 433, 490, 517, 525-39.

For the view that anorexia was the central metaphor of her life, see Gabriella Fiori, *Simone Weil: Une femme absolue* (Paris: Editions du Félin, 1987), 166-76.

29. See Bregman, "The Barren Fig Tree," 101, 113-14, where she writes of Weil's "mystical self-annihilation" in positive terms, and Dietz, *Between the Human and the Divine*, 189-95, which connects her patriotic effort to cure France with her spiritual self-sacrifice. See also Rees, *Simone Weil: A Sketch for a Portrait*, 54-56, where he refutes critics who attribute her self-immolating tendency to sex-repression.

30. See also *Notebooks*, 61, 84, 103, 134, 148, 160, 179, 181, 191, 193, 204, 207-8, 210-14, 217, 219, 221, 229, 234-36, 249, 258, 263, 266, 268, 272, 282, 284, 288, 292, 298-99, 312-13, 342, 359, 403, 411, 429, 474.

31. See McFarland, *Simone Weil*, 144. Cf. Karl Rahner, S.J., "Reflections on the Experience of Grace," *Theological Investigations* 3, trans. Karl-H. and Boniface Kruger (New York: Seabury Press, 1956), 86-90; and "The Man with the Pierced Heart," *Servants of the Lord*, trans. Richard Strachan (New York: Herder and Herder, 1968), 107-19. Cf. Annice Callahan, R.S.C.J., *Karl Rahner's Spirituality of the Pierced Heart: A Reinterpretation of Devotion to the Sacred Heart* (Lanham, Md.: University Press of America, 1985).

32. See Karl Rahner, *Everyday Faith*, trans. W. J. O'Hara (New York: Herder and Herder, 1968), 193-204; *The Love of Jesus and the Love of Neighbor*, trans. Robert Barr (New York: Crossroad, 1983), pp. 63-104; and *Visions and Prophecies*, Quaestiones Disputatae 10, trans. Charles Henkey and Richard Strachan (New York: Herder and Herder, 1964), 14, n.12.

33. See Blum and Seidler, *A Truer Liberty*, 304. For an example of a liberationist spirituality, see Gustavo Gutiérrez, *We Drink from Our Own Wells: The Spiritual Journey of a People*, trans. Matthew J. O'Connell (Maryknoll, N.Y.: Orbis, 1988). On the feminist concern for a relationship between spirituality and politics, see Jo Garcia and Sara Maitland, eds., *Walking on the Water: Women Talk about Spirituality* (London: Virago, 1983).

34. For this term, I am indebted to Roger Haight, S.J., "Liberationist Spirituality," in *An Alternative Vision: An Interpretation of Liberation Theology* (New York: Paulist, 1985), 233-56.

35. For example, see Thich Nhat Hanh, *The Miracle of Mindfulness: A Manual on Meditation*, trans. Mobi Warren (Boston: Beacon Press, 1976); and Lucy Lidell, *The Sivananda Companion to Yoga* (New York: Simon & Schuster, Fireside, 1983).

5. THOMAS MERTON
A Living Mystery of Solitude

Action	Thomas Merton, *Contemplation in a World of Action* (Garden City, N.Y.: Doubleday, Image, 1973).
Conjectures	Thomas Merton, *Conjectures of a Guilty Bystander* (Garden City, N.Y.: Doubleday, 1966).
CW	*Catholic Worker.*
Direction	Thomas Merton, *Spiritual Direction and Meditation* (Collegeville, Minn.: Liturgical Press, 1960).
Jonas	Thomas Merton *The Sign of Jonas* (Garden City, N.Y.: Doubleday, Image, 1960).
New Seeds	Thomas Merton, *New Seeds of Contemplation* (New York: New Directions, 1961).
Prayer	Thomas Merton, *Contemplative Prayer* (Garden City, N.Y.: Doubleday, Image, 1971).
Seeds	Thomas Merton, *Seeds of Contemplation* (New York: Dell, 1949).
Seven	Thomas Merton, *The Seven Storey Mountain* (New York: Harcourt Brace Jovanovich, Harvest, 1976).

1. See *Seven*, 281-82, 410-13. On his desire to be a Carthusian, see *Jonas*, 27; see also his correspondence with Dom Humphrey Pawsey in *The School of Charity: The Letters of Thomas Merton on Religious Renewal and Spiritual Direction*, ed. Patrick Hart, O.C.S.O. (New York: Farrar, Straus & Giroux, 1990), 13-14, 39-41.

On his struggle to be both monk and writer, see, for example, his correspondence with Dom Gabriel Sortais, *The School of Charity*.

2. For his reflections on solitude in *Jonas*, see 27-28, 70-71, 74, 80, 101, 116-17, 167-77, 229, 234, 243, 260-62, 301-2, 323, 326, 347. See also Merton, "The Inner Experience," *Cistercian Studies* 18-19 (1983-84); *No Man Is an Island* (Garden City, N.Y.: Doubleday, Image, 1967); "Notes for a Philosophy of Solitude," *Disputed Questions* (New York: Farrar, Straus & Cudahy, 1960), 177-207; *Thoughts in Solitude* (New York: Dell, 1961); *Thomas Merton in Alaska* (New York: New Directions, 1989), 42-44, 48-49, 58; *A Vow of Conversation: Journals 1964–1965*, ed. Naomi Burton Stone (New York: Farrar, Straus & Giroux, 1988), 6, 17, 18, 20, 53, 60, 88, 92, 107, 109-11, 120, 129, 136, 142, 144-45, 154-55, 171, 188, 190, 192, 198, 201-2, 204, 206. Cf. Raymond Bailey, *Thomas Merton on Mysticism* (Garden City, N.Y.: Doubleday, 1975), 53-187; Richard Anthony Cashen, *Solitude in the Thought of Thomas Merton* Cistercian Studies 40 (Kalamazoo, Mich.: Cistercian Publications, 1981); and John F. Teahan, "The Place of Silence in Thomas Merton's Life and Thought," *Journal of Religion* 61 (1981): 364-83.

3. See *Jonas*, 339–52; *Conjectures*, 212–14. Cf. David D. Cooper, *Thomas Merton's Art of Denial: The Evolution of a Radical Humanist* (Athens, Ga: University of Georgia Press, 1989), 192–226, esp. 205–6; and George A. Kilcourse, "Incarnation as the Integrative Principle in Thomas Merton's Poetry and Spirituality," dissertation, Fordham, 1974.

4. See Monica Furlong, *Merton: A Biography* (San Francisco: Harper & Row, 1980), 173.

5. See *Conjectures*, 131–32, 151, 158, 160, 271. He borrows this phrase from Louis Massignon. Cf. M. Madeleine Abdelnour, S.C.N., " '*Le point vierge*' in Thomas Merton," *Cistercian Studies* 6 (1971): 153–71; and Sidney H. Griffith, I.C.O.R., "Thomas Merton, Louis Massignon, and the Challenge of Islam," paper presented at the First International Thomas Merton Society General Meeting, Louisville, Kentucky, May 26, 1989.

6. Thomas Merton, "Apologies to an Unbeliever," *Faith and Violence: Christian Teaching and Christian Practice* (Notre Dame: University of Notre Dame Press, 1968), 213.

7. Thomas Merton, Preface to Japanese edition of *The Seven Storey Mountain*, in *Honorable Reader: Reflections on My Work*, ed. Robert E. Daggy (New York: Crossroad, 1989), 63. Cf. Norman King, "A Study in Solitude and Compassion," *Canadian Catholic Review* 3 (September 1985): 285–86; and Gerald Twomey, C.S.P., "Thomas Merton: An Appreciation," in *Thomas Merton: Prophet in the Belly of a Paradox*, ed. Gerald Twomey (New York: Paulist, 1978), 1–14.

8. See Paul Wilkes, ed., *Merton by Those Who Knew Him Best* (San Francisco: Harper & Row, 1984), 119–20.

9. See Cooper, *Thomas Merton's Art of Denial*, 166–91.

10. See Michael Mott, *The Seven Mountains of Thomas Merton* (Boston: Houghton Mifflin, 1984).

11. See Furlong, *Merton: A Biography*, 59–62.

12. See John Howard Griffin, *The Hermitage Journals: A Diary Kept while Working on the Biography of Thomas Merton*, ed. Congar Beasley, Jr. (Garden City, N.Y.: Doubleday, Image, 1983). See also John Howard Griffin, *Follow the Ecstasy: Thomas Merton, The Hermitage Years 1965–1968* (Fort Worth, Tex.: JHG Editions, Latitudes Press, 1983), and Mott, *The Seven Mountains of Thomas Merton*, 435–68.

13. See Thomas Merton, *The New Man* (New York: Farrar, Straus & Giroux, 1978).

14. See William H. Shannon, *Thomas Merton's Dark Path: The Inner Experience of a Contemplative* (New York: Farrar, Straus & Giroux, 1981), 156. Cf. Walter Conn, "Merton's 'True Self': Moral Autonomy and Religious Conversion," *Journal of Religion* 65 (1985): 513–29.

15. See Merton, "The Inner Experience," *Cistercian Studies*, especially the first two parts in this series of eight articles; and selections in Shannon, *Thomas Merton's Dark Path*, 114–41. Cf. Anne E. Carr, *A Search for Wisdom and Spirit: Thomas Merton's Theology of the Self* (Notre Dame: University of Notre Dame Press, 1988), 52.

16. See *Seeds*, 180–90; *New Seeds*, 275–89. Cf. Carr, *A Search for Wisdom*

and Spirit, 10–33; and John J. Higgins, S.J., *Thomas Merton on Prayer* (Garden City, N.Y.: Doubleday, 1973), 48–70.

17. See Merton, *Woods, Shore, Desert, A Notebook, May 1968* (Santa Fe, N.M.: Museum of New Mexico Press, 1982), 48. Cf. Thomas Del Prete, *Thomas Merton and the Education of the Whole Person* (Birmingham, Ala.: Religious Education Press, 1990), esp. chap. 3., "Self-Discovery as the Purpose of Education," 30–64.

18. See *The Hidden Ground of Love: The Letters of Thomas Merton on Religious Experience and Social Concerns*, ed. William H. Shannon (New York: Farrar, Straus & Giroux, 1985), 564.

19. See Thomas Merton, *Life and Holiness* (New York: Herder & Herder, 1963), 114–35.

20. See Elena Malits, C.S.C., *The Solitary Explorer: Thomas Merton's Transforming Journey* (San Francisco: Harper & Row, 1980), esp. 1–20, 139–56.

21. See *Direction*, 5–6, 8–9, 16, 20, 22, 24, 29–31.

22. Wilkes, *Merton by Those Who Knew Him Best*, 36.

23. One can pinpoint stages in his search for freedom. See Basil Pennington, *The Brother Monk: The Quest for True Freedom* (San Francisco: Harper & Row, 1987), esp. 38. On his spirituality, see Harvey D. Egan, S.J., chap. 6, "Thomas Merton (1915–1968)," in *Christian Mysticism: The Future of a Tradition* (New York: Pueblo, 1984), 215–59; and Charles J. Healey, S.J., "Thomas Merton (1915–1968)," in *Modern Spiritual Writers: Their Legacies of Prayer* (Staten Island, N.Y.: Alba House, 1989), 47–70.

24. Thomas Merton, *The Road to Joy: The Letters of Thomas Merton to New and Old Friends*, ed. Robert Daggy (New York: Farrar, Straus & Giroux, 1989), 163.

25. James T. Baker, *Thomas Merton: Social Critic* (Lexington, Ky.: University Press of Kentucky, 1971), 54; see also 1–43.

26. See also *Conjectures*, 53, 69–70, 81–83, 97–98, 326.

27. See "The Root of War," *CW* (October 1961): 1, 7–8; "The Root of War Is Fear," *Seeds*, 64–67, and *New Seeds*, 112–22.

28. See "The Shelter Ethic," *CW* 28 (November 1961), 1, 5; "Advice to a Young Prophet," *CW* 28 (January 1962): 4; "Thomas Merton on the Strike," *CW* 28 (February 1962): 7; "Christian Ethics and Nuclear War," *CW* 28 (March 1962): 2, 7; "Ethics and War, A Footnote," *CW* 28 (April 1962): 2; "We Have to Make Ourselves Heard," *CW* 28 (May 1962): 4–6; "We Have to Make Ourselves Heard-Continued," *CW* 28 (June 1962): 4–5.

See also Merton, "Nuclear War and Christian Responsibility," *Commonweal* 75 (February 19, 1962): 509–13; *A Thomas Merton Reader*, ed. Thomas P. McDonnell (New York: Harcourt, Brace & World, 1962), 288, 293–94, 301–2.

29. See *Conjectures*, 271. See also Thomas Merton, "An Open Letter to the American Hierarchy: Schema XIII and the Modern World," *Worldview* 8 (September 1965): 4–7; and *Breakthrough to Peace* (Norfolk, Conn.: J. Laughlin, 1962), 108.

30. See Thomas Merton, "Christian Morality and Nuclear War," *Way* 19 (June 1963): 12–22; *A Thomas Merton Reader*, 288–305; Thomas Merton, *Orig-*

inal Child Bomb (New York: New Directions, 1961), 1-15; and *Breakthrough to Peace.* Cf. Baker, *Thomas Merton: Social Critic,* 44-97.

31. See Merton, *Faith and Violence,* 3-84, and *Thomas Merton on Peace* (New York: McCall, 1971), 166-253. Cf. Cooper, *Thomas Merton's Art of Denial,* 227-69.

On the influence of Gandhi, see Thomas Merton, ed., *Gandhi on Non-Violence* (New York: New Directions, 1965).

On the futility and brutality of war, see Thomas Merton, *My Argument with the Gestapo: A Macaronic Journal* (Garden City, N.Y.: Doubleday, 1969).

On the silent collusion of Adolf Eichmann, see Thomas Merton, *Raids on the Unspeakable* (New York: New Directions, 1964), 45-62. See also *Conjectures,* 285-90; and "Epitaph for a Public Servant," *The Collected Poems of Thomas Merton* (New York: New Directions, 1977), 705.

On his solidarity with Thich Nhat Hanh, the Vietnamese Zen Buddhist pacifist monk, see Merton, "Nhat Hanh Is My Brother," in *Thomas Merton on Peace,* 262-63; and *Mystics & Zen Masters* (New York: Dell, Delta, 1969), 285-88. Cf. James H. Forest, "Thomas Merton's Struggle with Peacemaking," in *Thomas Merton: Prophet in the Belly of a Paradox,* 15-54, esp. 48-50.

32. See Thomas Merton, "A Letter to Pablo Antonio Cuadra concerning Giants," *Emblems of a Season of Fury* (New York: New Directions, 1963), 70-89.

For examples of the connections concerning militarism, racism, sexism, and classism, see Joanna Rogers Macy, *Despair and Personal Power in the Nuclear Age* (Philadelphia: New Society, 1983), and Sharon D. Welch, *The Feminist Ethic of Risk* (Minneapolis: Fortress Press, 1990).

33. Merton, "Author's Note," *Seeds of Destruction* (New York: Farrar, Straus & Giroux, 1964), xiv-xv. Cf. Thomas Merton, "Preface to the Spanish edition of *Seeds of Destruction:* A Christmas Letter 1965," in *Introductions East and West: The Foreign Prefaces of Thomas Merton,* ed. Robert E. Daggy (Greensboro: Unicorn Press, 1981), 81-86.

34. See *Prayer.* Cf. Carr, *A Search for Wisdom and Spirit,* 108-20.

35. *Prayer,* 101. See also 97, 100; and "The Inner Experience," esp. the third and last of the series of eight articles.

36. See Ross Labrie, *The Art of Thomas Merton* (Fort Worth: Texas Christian University Press, 1979), esp. 1-25. Cf. Annice Callahan, R.S.C.J., "Creative Intuition as Analogous to Contemplative Intuition," *RSCJ: A Journal of Reflection* 2 (1980): 77-88.

37. For example, see Therese Lentfoehr, *Words and Silence: On the Poetry of Thomas Merton* (New York: New Directions, 1979); and *A Merton Concelebration,* ed. Deba Prasad Patnaik (Notre Dame: Ave Maria, 1981). Cf. Victor A. Kramer, *Thomas Merton* (Boston: Twayne, 1984), 33-53.

38. See Merton, "Sacred Art and the Spiritual Life," *Disputed Questions,* 151-64; and "Notes on Sacred Art," conferences to the Novices, Gethsemani Abbey. Cf. John Howard Griffin, *A Hidden Wholeness: The Visual World of Thomas Merton* (Boston: Houghton Mifflin, 1970); *Geography of Holiness: The Photography of Thomas Merton,* ed. Deba Patnaik (New York: Pilgrim Press, 1980).

39. For example, see *Jonas,* 54, 56, 61, 102-3, 107, 204-5, 235, 245-47. Cf.

Cooper, *Thomas Merton's Art of Denial,* 15–60; and Victor Kramer, "Thomas Merton's Published Journals: The Paradox of Writing as a Step toward Contemplation," *Studia Mystica* 3 (1980): 3–20.

40. See Merton, *Zen and the Birds of Appetite* (New York: New Directions, 1968), 75–77.

41. See Patrick Hart, O.C.S.O., Intro., *The Message of Thomas Merton,* Cistercian Studies 42 (Kalamazoo, Mich.: Cistercian Publications, 1981), 8. Cf. Karl Rahner, S.J., *Visions and Prophecies,* Quaestiones Disputatae 10, trans. Charles Henkey and Richard Strachan (New York: Herder & Herder, 1964), 14, n. 12.

42. See K. Rahner, *The Love of Jesus and the Love of Neighbor,* trans. Robert Barr (New York: Crossroad, 1983), 63–104.

43. See Annice Callahan, R.S.C.J., *Karl Rahner's Spirituality of the Pierced Heart: A Reinterpretation of Devotion to the Sacred Heart* (Lanham, Md.: University Press of America, 1985), 90–100.

44. For example, see Karl Rahner, S.J., *On Prayer* (New York: Paulist, Deus, 1968), esp. 45–55, and *Everyday Faith,* trans. W. J. O'Hara (New York: Herder & Herder, 1968), 193–204.

45. On his contribution to monasticism, see, for example, his correspondence with Dom Jean Leclerq, O.S.B., in *The School of Charity;* Jean Leclerq, O.S.B., "The Evolving Monk," in *Thomas Merton/Monk: A Monastic Tribute,* ed. Patrick Hart, O.C.S.O. (New York: Sheed & Ward, 1974), 93–104; and Jean Leclerq, Introduction, *Contemplation in a World of Action,* 7–18.

On his compulsion to write, see Malits, *The Solitary Explorer,* 142–47.

On his decision to remain a Cistercian, see *Jonas,* 20, 67–68, 102, 127, 139, 244; and *Conjectures,* 183, 258. Cf. Frederic Joseph Kelly, S.J., *Man before God: Thomas Merton on Social Responsibility* (Garden City, N.Y.: Doubleday, 1974), 58–59; Bailey, *Thomas Merton on Mysticism,* 60, 62, 82; and John Eudes Bamberger, O.C.S.O., "The Monk," in *Thomas Merton/Monk: A Monastic Tribute,* 37–58. For an opposite view, see Edward Rice, *The Man in the Sycamore Tree: The Good Times and Hard Life of Thomas Merton* (Garden City, N.Y.: Doubleday, Image, 1970), 124.

46. See Frederic J. Kelly, S.J., "A Prophetic Struggle toward Freedom and Social Responsibility," *Christian Spirituality in the United States: Independence and Interdependence,* ed. Francis A. Eigo, O.S.A. (Villanova, Pa.: Villanova University Press, 1978), 174–75.

47. See Merton, "Monastic Experience and East-West Dialogue," *The Asian Journal of Thomas Merton,* ed. Naomi Burton et al. (New York: New Directions, 1975), 312–13.

48. Malits, *The Solitary Explorer,* 155.

49. On the sense in which he can be called a theologian, see Carr, *A Search for Wisdom and Spirit,* 3–7; and Lawrence S. Cunningham, "Thomas Merton: The Pursuit of Marginality," *Christian Century* 95 (December 6, 1978): 1183.

6. HENRI NOUWEN
Prophet of Conversion

Beauty	Henri Nouwen, *Behold the Beauty of the Lord: Praying with Icons* (Notre Dame: Ave Maria Press, 1987).
Cry	Henri Nouwen, *A Cry for Mercy: Prayers from the Genesee* (Garden City, N.Y.: Doubleday, Image, 1983).
Genesee	Henri Nouwen, *Genesee Diary: Report from a Trappist Monastery* (Garden City, N.Y.: Doubleday, 1976).
Healer	Henri Nouwen, *The Wounded Healer: Ministry in Contemporary Society* (Garden City, N.Y.: Doubleday, 1972), 87.
Intimacy	Henri Nouwen, *Intimacy: Pastoral Psychological Essays* (Notre Dame: Fides, 1969).
Love	Henri Nouwen, *Canvas of Love: Reflections on a Rembrandt* (Garden City, N.Y.: Doubleday, forthcoming), unpublished manuscript.
Merton	Henri Nouwen, *Thomas Merton: Contemplative Critic* (San Francisco: Harper & Row, 1981).
Ministry	Henri Nouwen, *Creative Ministry* (Garden City, N.Y.: Doubleday, Image, 1978).
Mirror	Henri Nouwen *Beyond the Mirror: Reflections on Death and Life* (New York: Crossroad, 1990).
New	Henri Nouwen, *Making All Things New: An Invitation to the Spiritual Life* (San Francisco: Harper & Row, 1981).
Reaching	Henri Nouwen, *Reaching Out: The Three Movements of the Spiritual Life* (Garden City, N.Y.: Doubleday, 1975), 139.
Rome	Henri Nouwen, *Clowning in Rome: Reflections on Solitude, Celibacy, Prayer, and Contemplation* (Garden City, N.Y.: Doubleday, Image, 1979).
Walk	Henri Nouwen, *Walk with Jesus: Stations of the Cross* (Maryknoll, N.Y.: Orbis, 1990).
Way	Henri Nouwen, *The Way of the Heart* (New York: Ballantine Book, 1981).

1. See Bernard J. F. Lonergan, S.J., *Method in Theology* (New York: Herder and Herder, 1973), 237–44; Robert Doran, S.J., "Jungian Psychology and Christian Spirituality," *Review for Religious*, 38 (1979): 4/497–510, 5/742–52, 6/857–66; and *Subject and Psyche: Ricoeur, Jung, and the Search for Foundations* (Washington, D.C.: University Press of America, 1977), esp. 240–46.

Cf. Walter E. Conn, ed., *Conversion: Perspectives on Personal and Social Transformation* (Staten Island, N.Y.: Alba House, 1978).

2. See Brian O. McDermott, S.J., *What Are They Saying about the Grace of Christ?* (New York: Paulist, 1984), esp. 21–34.

3. See Paul V. Robb, S.J., "Conversion as a Human Experience," *Studies in the Spirituality of Jesuits* 14 (May 1982): 1–50.

4. See Paul Tillich, *The Shaking of the Foundations* (New York: Charles Scribner's Sons, 1948), 160–63.

5. For a summary of Nouwen's spirituality of the heart describing his approach to solitude, service, prayer, compassion, gratitude, and communion, see Annice Callahan, R.S.C.J., "Henri Nouwen: The Heart as Home," *Spiritualities of the Heart: Approaches to Personal Wholeness in Christian Tradition*, ed. Annice Callahan (New York: Paulist, 1990), 201–17.

6. Robert Durback, "Henri Nouwen: Spirituality for a Technological Age," *Praying* 18 (May–June 1987): 10.

7. See Henri Nouwen, *The Road to Daybreak: A Spiritual Journey* (New York: Doubleday, 1988).

8. See ibid., 46, 58, 60, 64–69, 81, 113–14, 153, 174.

9. On his call to self-acceptance, see ibid., 46, 58, 60, 64–69, 81, 113–14, 153, 174. On his call to prayer, see 73–74, 116–17, 133, 184, 207, 226, 147–48, 180, 209, 211, 213, 218. On l'Arche's gospel values, see 38, 62, 192.

10. For example, he was drawn to pray before icons during three of his visits to l'Arche in Trosly, France. See *Beauty*.

11. See also *Mirror*, 12, 51, 54, 60, 62, 74.

12. See Henri Nouwen, series of articles on peacemaking, *New Oxford Review* 52 (September 1985): 7–18; (October 1985): 10–18; and (November 1985): 19–26.

13. Henri Nouwen, *With Open Hands* (Notre Dame: Ave Maria, 1972), 154.

14. Henri Nouwen and Walter J. Gaffney, *Aging: The Fulfillment of Life* (Garden City, N.Y.: Doubleday, Image, 1976), 117.

From his books *In Memoriam* (Notre Dame: Ave Maria Press, 1980) and *A Letter of Consolation* (San Francisco: Harper & Row, 1980), one sees clearly that Nouwen has been with his parents in their aging process and can empathize with the guilt, frustration, gratitude, and fear of others who care for their aging parents. He has allowed these moments to become part of his conversion process.

15. See Henri Nouwen, *From Resentment to Gratitude* (Chicago: Franciscan Herald Press, 1974).

16. See Henri Nouwen, *The Living Reminder: Service and Prayer in Memory of Jesus Christ* (New York: Seabury, Crossroad, 1977). On prayer and ministry, see also Nouwen, *Rome*, 18–24, 85–108; and *Way*, 63–70.

17. See Henri Nouwen, "The Monk and the Cripple: Toward a Spirituality of Ministry," *America* 142 (March 15, 1980): 205–10.

18. See Henri Nouwen, "Living the Questions: The Spirituality of the Religion Teacher," *Union Seminary Quarterly Review* 32 (Fall 1976): 17–24.

19. See Henri Nouwen, "Theology as Doxology: Reflections on Theological Education," in *Caring for the Commonweal: Education for Religious and Public*

Life, ed. Parker J. Palmer, Barbara G. Wheeler, and James W. Fowler (Macon, Ga.: Mercer University Press, 1990), 93–109, esp. 93–101.

20. Ibid., 107. See also 101–9.

21. On conversion, see also *Intimacy,* 29, and *Cry,* 64.

22. See Henri Nouwen, "Spiritual Direction," *Worship* 55 (September 1981): 399–404, reprinted as *Spiritual Direction* (Cincinnati: Forward Movement Publications, 1981).

23. See Henri Nouwen, "A Sudden Trip to Lourdes," *New Oxford Review* 57 (September 1990): 7–13. On Mary's mediating role in Nouwen's and our conversion process, see also *Genesee,* 62–64, 90–91; *In Memoriam,* 53; *A Letter of Consolation,* 73; *Beauty,* 31–42; *Walk,* 27–29.

24. Nouwen, "Our True Spiritual Identity," National Catholic Education Association Opening Session, Convention Center, Toronto, April 17, 1990, tape.

25. See Donald P. McNeill, Douglas A. Morrison, and Henri Nouwen, *Compassion: A Reflection on the Christian Life* (Garden City, N.Y.: Doubleday, Image, 1983), 64.

26. See Henri Nouwen, *Gracias! A Latin American Journal* (San Francisco: Harper & Row, 1983).

27. See Henri Nouwen, *Love in a Fearful Land: A Guatemala Story* (Notre Dame: Ave Maria Press, 1985).

28. Henri Nouwen, *Lifesigns: Intimacy, Fecundity, and Ecstasy in Christian Perspective* (Garden City, N.Y.: Doubleday, Image, 1986), 48.

29. See Mary Frances Coady, "Nouwen Finds Rest at Daybreak," *Catholic New Times,* November 23, 1986, 4.

30. See Henri Nouwen, "Case-Recording in Pastoral Education," *Journal of the Academy of Parish Clergy* 4 (September. 1974), 16–24; "Boisen and the Case Method," *Chicago Theological Seminary Register: A Professional Journal for Ministers* 67 (Winter 1977): 12–32; and "Anton T. Boisen and Theology through Living Human Documents," *Pastoral Psychology* 19 (September 1968): 49–63. In this regard, I think Nouwen relies on Boisen's use of the case study method in clinical pastoral education as a model for teaching spirituality through living human documents. Nouwen uses his own life story and the life stories of others as his laboratory where he teaches his readers the science of the heart. So, in effect, he uses stories as "case studies."

31. Peter T. Rohrbach, review of *Reaching Out* by Nouwen, *America* 7 (June 1975): 448.

32. See John S. Mogabgab, "The Spiritual Pedagogy of Henri Nouwen," *Yale Divinity School Reflection* (January 1981): 4–6. Nouwen was named "Pastoral Theologian of the Year" in 1978 by the journal *Pastoral Psychology* and has become increasingly famous for his "creative-encounter" approach to theological education. See Seward Hiltner, "Henri Nouwen: Pastoral Theologian of the Year," *Pastoral Psychology* 27 (Fall 1978): 5.

33. See Robert Bellah et al., *Habits of the Heart: Individualism and Commitment in American Life* (San Francisco: Harper & Row, 1985). Cf. Allan Bloom, *The Closing of the American Mind* (New York: Simon and Schuster, 1987).

34. See Henri Nouwen, *In the Name of Jesus* (New York: Crossroad, 1989).

35. Nouwen, *Genesee*, 59, 157–59, 187, written in 1974 during his first stay at the Genesee, and *Cry*, in which during his second stay at the Genesee in 1979 he addresses his daily written prayer to Christ, begging for a closeness to Christ. See also the monthly installments of his Trosly-Breuil journal in *New Oxford Review* 53 (September–December 1986) and 54 (January–June 1987) in which he often writes of desiring and experiencing closeness to Jesus, both at l'Arche and on trips he took during that time. Cf. Joan Frawley, "Henri Nouwen: A Physician of the Heart, Himself Healed," *National Catholic Register* (December 21, 1986), 1, 9, which attests that by this time he seems to be listening more to his mother's voice assuring him he is loved and only needs to love Jesus, than to his father's voice feeding his ambition for success. For examples of the simplicity of his relationship with Jesus, see Henri Nouwen, *Letters to Mark* (San Francisco: Harper & Row, 1988), and *Heart Speaks to Heart* (Notre Dame: Ave Maria Press, 1988).

36. For example, a book reviewer in the United States wrote: "Nouwen's personal life and his reflections upon his experiences have served as a catalyst for renewal in this country." See Betty W. Talbert, "Books: *The Way of the Heart*," *Mission Journal* (August 1982): 19.

37. See Karl Rahner, "Reflections on the Experience of Grace," *Theological Investigations* 3, trans. Karl-H. and Boniface Kruger (New York: Seabury, Crossroad, 1974), 86–90.

On a mysticism of everyday life, see Karl Rahner, *Belief Today: Theological Meditations*, ed. Hans Küng, trans. M. H. Healan (New York: Sheed and Ward, 1967), 13–43; and *Everyday Faith*, trans. W. J. O'Hara (New York: Herder & Herder, 1968), 193–204.

See also Karl Rahner, "The Man with the Pierced Heart," *Servants of the Lord*, trans. Richard Strachan (New York: Herder & Herder, 1968), 107–19. Cf. Annice Callahan, *Karl Rahner's Spirituality of the Pierced Heart: Toward a Reinterpretation of Devotion to the Sacred Heart* (Lanham, Md.: University Press of America, 1985).

Epilogue

1. For a provocative and critical reflection on traditional metaphors and practices of the Christian life, see Margaret R. Miles, *Practicing Christianity: Critical Perspectives for an Embodied Spirituality* (New York: Crossroad, 1988), esp. 176–84.

2. See William Callahan, S.J., *Noisy Contemplation* (Washington, D.C.: Quixote Center, 1983); and "Noisy Contemplation: Is Prayer in a Busy Life?" *New Theology Review* 2 (1989): 29–39.

3. See Elizabeth Dreyer, *Manifestations of Grace* (Wilmington, Del.: Michael Glazier, 1990), esp. 236–40.

Index